DOM ANTÔNIO B. FRAGOSO

FACE OF A CHURCH

A Nascent Church of the People
in Crateús, Brazil

*Translated from the Portuguese
By Robert R. Barr*

ORBIS BOOKS
Maryknoll, New York 10545

Originally published as *O rosto de uma igreja,* © 1982 by Edições Loyola, Rua 1822 no. 347, Caixa Postal 42.335, São Paulo, Brasil

English translation © 1987 by Orbis Books, Maryknoll, NY 10545
All rights reserved
Manufactured in the United States of America

Manuscript editor: William E. Jerman

Library of Congress Cataloging-in-Publication Data

Fragoso, Antônio Batista, 1920-
  Face of the church.

  Translation of: O rosto de uma igreja.
  1. Catholic Church—Brazil—Crateús. 2. Crateús
(Brazil)—Religious life and customs.—I. Title.
BX1467.C68F7313   1987   282'.8131   87-14205
ISBN 0-88344-576-X
ISBN 0-88344-551-4 (pbk.)

CONTENTS

iii

PART THREE
THE WITNESS OF CO-WORKERS   125

FOREWORD

*Creuza Maciel, General Coordinator of SERPAJ-AL
(Service of Peace and Justice in Latin America)*

THE DIOCESE OF CRATEÚS

Many articles and books have been written *about* base ecclesial communities and about the church of the poor. This book, however, was written *by* people who have worked—some for over twenty years—to build a church of the people in one diocese, the diocese of Crateús, in the Northeast of Brazil. The book is the story of a diocese struggling to side with the poor in the context of crushing poverty. Part of the story is told by the bishop, Bishop Antônio Fragoso, and part of the story is told by sisters and priests living with the poor of the diocese, by advisors to the base communities, and by others involved in building a church from the grassroots, the people, upward. The book has a humble goal, it is utterly local: in many places it gives the details of day-to-day pastoral work in the diocese. It is, in short, an inside look at the process of building a church of the people in a particular place. It is about the kind of church that is the source of liberation theology.

To help readers enter the world of the diocese of Crateús, I want to first say a few words about that diocese and about the background of my involvement with it. The diocese was begun in the 1960s—1964 to be exact. During that time I lived not far from Crateús. I was working as a sister and participating actively in a church that was caught between the cries of the poor and its European traditions of legalism, aristocracy, and centralized power. The suffering and despair of the people had begun to convert a part of that church, which gradually took its stand with the poor and sought specific forms of commitment alongside the people. During that part of the 1960s Vatican II was underway, and the doors of the church were opened to let in fresh air. People began to hear the Holy Spirit through the hunger and the cry of the oppressed and the starving, and church officeholders were pressed to take a concrete stand.

The diocese of Crateús is one of those in Brazil that has taken the leadership in the search for a clear commitment alongside the poor. It has done this in a very poor region—Crateús, in 1987 its population being about 480,000, is one of the poorest states in Brazil. It has done this in a region where people live in slavery and are condemned not only to disease and early death, but also to social and cultural death. From that context a new church began to arise, one that expresses itself as a people, that lives and works with the people, that respects the people's culture and becomes a part of it.

THE BOOK, ITS AUTHORS, AND THEIR COMMUNITY

Face of a Church is the expression of a church made up of women and men who are hungry and exploited—men and women who are facing the challenge of liberation as a demand of their faith. This book is the expression of a church searching for its own identity, and thus it is a work of self-criticism. As the people of the diocese, as the priests, religious, and layworkers, and as the bishop review the more that twenty years of history of their diocese, they confront questions such as these: How are we to be church in the midst of a people that is hungry, assaulted, impoverished, smashed down? What does our church look like? What is our identity? These and other questions have arisen from within this diocesan community, and the answers have emerged in the form of this book.

The book is divided into three parts. In the first, more historical, part, Bishop Antônio Fragoso reconstructs from his own perspective the journey of God's people in the diocese of Crateús—with its advances and setbacks, its mistakes and successes. Bishop Fragoso focuses on a number of key problems and challenges. In Crateús more than twenty years have now been devoted to the difficult work of systematically recovering the dignity of the poor, decentralizing church power, creating communities, and raising the consciousness of the poor so that they themselves can be the builders of their own community of believers: so that they may believe in their own power and in the power of other poor people, especially when they are united and organized. The people's hunger is another problem that has confronted the diocese. How to deal with the problem of educating the people in the faith and celebrating the faith and trust in the God who is love when the life of these people is one of utter suffering caused by so much injustice, oppression, and death?

Just as great a challenge is the conversion of the bishop, the priests, the sisters, and others so that they will allow the people to make their own way, to accept the initiatives that come from their communities, to be open to popular culture, assimilate it, respect it . . . to live today's insecurity and tomorrow's uncertainty. . . . Thus in the first part of the book the bishop devotes considerable attention to this conversion process, which began when the diocese of Crateús turned its lands over to the poor. The diocese's lands were turned over to landless families or to community projects to help the communities survive economically and to prepare them for a more dignified life. That and other acts were but small steps in the life of the people, taken in order to nourish their confidence in their own ability and their hope as they make their way along. But Bishop Fragoso makes it clear that no one was deceived into thinking that those small acts would liberate the poor from the forces that oppress them. As the church in Crateús struggled to orient itself toward the poor, it became clearer and clearer that the reasons for the people's poverty were structural, and hence extremely complex. So in part 1 Bishop Fragoso discusses how the church confronted these problems—step by humble step.

In part 2 Bishop Fragoso pauses to take stock, to interpret the events he has discussed in part 1, inquiring what it means to be church and clearly revealing the profile of the church in Crateús. As a way of reflecting on what Bishop Fragoso says in part 2, I would like to focus on one representative issue that he deals with in that part. He discusses the issue of the popular church, its role and its relationship to the authorities of the Roman church. The so-called popular church has often been shunned, criticized, and even condemned, as is the case of the church of the people in Nicaragua. I believe the church in Crateús is more radical than the church in Nicaragua. While in the Nicaraguan church there is a separation between the hierarchy's way of life and that of the poor, in Crateús the people and the hierarchy stand within the same process. Indeed, the hierarchy is striving to become converted; it is approaching the poor to become incarnate in their situation, to become identified with their life and history. This is a church that gives up privileges, that gives up economic aid from outside; it is a church in which the bishop, the religious, and pastoral agents live on a minimum wage, about $35 per month. Some of them, a number of priests for example, actually live as simply as peasants, working the land. For his part, the bishop lives on a street in a poor neighborhood, in a house just like all the rest, without even a plaque to indicate that a bishop lives there. The door is open to take in whoever comes by, and those who come in can sit down at the table to eat whatever there is. This is a revolutionary way of being church; for this church does not just look like the people—it *is* the people. The reflections presented by Bishop Fragoso in this part of the book show the deep traces of a base-community diocese: they picture a church that is suffering, persecuted, poor, nonviolent, and therefore *holy*.

Finally, part 3 consists of "co-testimonials"—assessments of the identity of the church in Crateús written by priests and sisters who have been involved in the experience of building up a popular church in the diocese. These statements are crucial to the structure of the book for a number of reasons: (1) they give voice to those working at various levels of the diocese; some of the statements in part 3 were written by priests and sisters who have lived and worked for years among the poor, and they thus reflect many of the concerns of the poorest persons in the diocese; (2) having statements written by those who work at various levels in the diocese reflects one of the central concerns of the church of Crateús and its bishop: to shift the seat of power from the hierarchy to the poor; (3) Bishop Fragoso's statements in parts 1 and 2 are for the most part about the diocese as a whole, but the statements in part 3 often discuss specific issues that arise in the small communities, and that can be enlightening—an example being the Jesuits's discussions of the difficulties of working with base communities over which landowners have usurped control; and (4) for those interested in the details of the day-to-day pastoral work in a diocese that has sided with the poor, the statements offer detailed accounts of concrete problems and solutions related to specific programs and pedagogies used in the diocese at all levels.

Rather than comment further on what is said by those who participated in composing this book, it seems better for me simply to add my voice to theirs; for, as I said above, I began following the transformations in the diocese of Crateús when it was founded, and I have continued to be involved and keenly interested in the shaping of the church of the people in Crateús and elsewhere in the Northeast of Brazil. In what follows, then, I shall say something about my own experiences with and reflections on the shaping of that church.

Recently Bishop Fragoso invited me, along with my husband, to take part in the Crateús diocesan pastoral council meeting, which takes place every three months. The council is made up of the bishop, the priests who are in charge of parishes, representatives from different areas of work, sisters who are part of the diocese, and other pastoral agents—altogether about sixty people, mainly lay. Starting with a day of community recreational activities, the council members spend four days evaluating their work by programs and areas of activity. They engage in self-criticism; they discuss issues and problems; they study and go more deeply into particular issues in the life of the diocese and into other topics of interest to the group. They celebrate together, make decisions, and plan the activities of the diocese. There is a great deal of participation, in a climate of much trust and great joy: songs expressing the day-to-day life and speech of the people are a constant element throughout the pastoral council meeting.

This evaluation process, an integral part of the movement, is also a pedagogical process. It is pedagogical because it involves all the participants in studying a wide variety of topics and in completing a number of tasks. During each meeting, plans are made for the next meeting: tasks are divided up, enabling all to take part; individuals are chosen to coordinate the overall plan for the next meeting; representatives from different parishes and areas of work and from the base communities are chosen to engage in various types of study and work. Each delegate has a function, takes part in different commissions, and has a mandate from his or her own community or group.

The usual role of a bishop—and indeed of an entire diocesan

structure—becomes irrelevant to the kind of situation I am describing. Dom Fragoso is an older brother, one who stimulates with the witness of his faith and who provides the core of unity. In the meeting of the pastoral council, the bishop was never present in an authoritarian way, as the boss, the one with the last word. One scarcely heard the bishop speak. He made his presence felt more through his simplicity and fellow spirit than through the authority that usually attends a "princess of the church." Service is the trademark of a popular and liberating church.

I recall that one of the points under discussion at the council meeting was the project of building a refectory as part of the diocesan training center. A commission had previously prepared all the information needed for the discussion. In the discussion people assessed not only whether such a project was necessary and whether the money was available, but they also considered whether the creation of such structures would be consistent with the life they were leading. The point here is not the decision reached; it is the process—all in the diocese participating in making decisions. It is worth noting here that over fifteen years ago the diocese of Crateús decided not to ask for money from the outside. If friends in Europe or the United States send money on their own, such help is always welcome. All aid received is administered by a commission and how such resources will be used is decided during the pastoral commission meetings.

The evaluation deals not only with overall projects and specific programs but also with the diocese's stand on particular events and situations, such as agrarian reform, which is a basic issue in Brazil today. Sometimes there are heated discussions and harsh criticisms in the meetings, but mutual respect, a family spirit, freedom of expression for all, and the joint responsibility that bonds all in an atmosphere of mutual trust and friendship mean that, as tough as the evaluation might be, it stimulates people and gives them energy for moving ahead. Thus, day by day, a base-community diocese is being put together, and gradually it is opening the way for the future of the church of Jesus Christ in the present moment of the old and ever new history of God's people.

I am thankful to have been familiar with churches like the one in the diocese of Crateús; my personal experiences parallel much of what is in this book. I have spent most of my life in the Northeast of

Brazil as an active member of a church that became aware of its complicity in history with those who abused the poor but did not know for years how to turn that situation around. In trying to align that church with the poor, the initial experiences were very encouraging and inspiring. Of course there were criticisms, prohibitions, and pressures from within the church itself and particularly from those who held economic and military power. But life overcomes death. Some dioceses were able to pass through the ordeal of fire; others were paralyzed by fear or the inability to change; the leaders of still other dioceses consciously or unconsciously remain shut up in their palaces, confident that they are offering pleasing worship to God.

The experience of church concretely expressed in this book, an experience whose deep meaning is revealed through the words of Isaiah 49:6, "I will make you a light to the nations," leads us to believe in the power of the poor and in the Spirit of God who "makes all things new."

I believe that this translation of this book will inspire my English-speaking brothers and sisters who are seeking a way for making the kingdom of God something real in history. I believe that the profile of the church of Croteús contained in this work will stimulate those who are discouraged to believe in the power of the weak; will help guide the comfortable to find the uneasiness they need to venture out to build a living, community-oriented, and participatory church; will inspire the anguished so that they may find the hope to set up visible signs of justice and human dignity; and will challenge all men and women of good will to seek liberation at the present moment of history as a condition for full participation in the life brought by Jesus Christ (John 10:10).

RIO DE JANEIRO

Translated by Phillip Berryman

ACRONYMS

CEB, *Comunidade Eclesias de Base,* Base (Grassroots) Ecclesial Community

CNBB, *Conferência Nacional dos Bispos do Brasil,* National Conference of the Bishops of Brazil

CONTAG, *Confederação Nacional dos Trabahladores Agrícolas,* National Confederation of Farm Workers

CPT, *Comissão Pastoral da Terra,* Land Pastoral Commission

FINA, *Fundação Interamericana,* Inter-American Foundation

MEB, *Movimento de Educação de Base,* Basic Education Movement

SUDENE, *Superintendência de Desenvolvimento do Nordeste,* Superintendency for Development of the Northeast

PART ONE

A SIXTEEN-YEAR JOURNEY: THE STORY OF THE CHURCH IN CRATEÚS, BRAZIL

I arrived in the diocese of Crateús on August 8, 1964.

Since then, along with so many others, I have lived a story.

The story is not my own, then. It is the story of priests, nuns, and laity, militant and nonmilitant. It is the story of the practicing masses as I have found them.

But neither is it a story told by the diocese as a whole. It is a story as I see it, with my eyes. It is not a model for anyone to copy. It is the story of an attempt, a journey, a search for the kingdom of God, in my diocesan area.

We are all sisters and brothers. It will be a good thing if some of us hear what other brothers and sisters have lived and experienced, so that we may offer one another some help—with all our sins and limitations, but with our successes and hopes, too.

I take personal responsibility for what I say here. I do not wish to involve anyone else in the diocese in my testimony.

1

I ARRIVE IN CRATEÚS

It was a lovely afternoon, August 8, 1964.

I had come from the city of João Pessoa [some four hundred miles to the east, on the "shoulder" of Brazil that jutts out into the Atlantic Ocean].

In Pedra Branca, I had been received by the commandant of the Fourth Engineers Battalion, accompanied by his staff and by some other persons I did not know, representing the diocese.

I have always been something of a *camponês**—a little befuddled, clumsy, a little bit the hick—even though I have had opportunities in life that many others have not had. I could not have imagined that I would be so warmly welcomed.

In the rectory at Independência, Father José Jacques Moura offered his brotherly hospitality for supper, and that evening we set out for Crateús. I was received once more by the Fourth Engineers, with a cocktail party given by the commandant and other officials. Then for the first time in my life, I reviewed troops. That left me a little bewildered! I couldn't see just why I should be doing that. What had I done in my past that would merit homage like this?

---

* A *camponês* (plural, *camponeses*) (in Spanish, *campesino*) is someone who lives from the *campo,* the field, the land, but is not a landowner, except perhaps of a small plot insufficient to meet the needs of life. A *camponês* must therefore work for someone else, generally under gruelling conditions and for substandard wages. *Camponês* and *campesino* are sometimes translated "peasant."

Then I went by car to the city, where I was cheered by a large crowd, while a son of the soil cast flower petals on our heads from a helicopter.

At the cathedral steps a reviewing stand had been set up for the arriving bishop and city dignitaries. There was really a crowd there. Ceará is a state where persons resonate with an unusual public event, when the spirit moves them.

Present were the archbishop of Fortaleza, José de Medeiros Delgado, whose auxiliary I had been in São Luís do Maranhão, several other bishops, the clergy, Governor Virgílio Távora, and all the local authorities.

2

FRUSTRATED EXPECTATIONS

I was met by Claudino Sales—"Dr. Salim," as we call him—who eventually became a state deputy, secretary of the state of Ceará, president of the Ceará Legislative Assembly, and a federal deputy. He owned the only industry in Crateús.

Dr. Salim greeted me with effusive expressions of joy and kindness. With the collaboration of Bishop José Tupinambá da Frota (the bishop of Sobral, which had included eight of the ten parishes of the new Crateús diocese), he had made Sobral famous, building schools, hospitals, museums, orphanages, asylums. He was a real "builder of civilization," and he hoped that the new bishop, Antônio Batista Fragoso, would be a "builder of civilization" in Crateús.

Rather high hopes awaited the arriving bishop.

I was to give a reply. I thought it my duty to give one that I knew would be undiplomatic and very frustrating to the expectations of members of the welcoming party.

I thanked the group, from the bottom of my heart, for the homage they were doing me. But I said I wanted to be honest and sincere with them. As regards construction initiatives, the bishop of Crateús would not be following in the footsteps of the beloved bishop of Sobral, José Tupinambá da Frota! He would not be a "builder of civilization." He would not build a university, a school, a hospital, or first-aid station. First and foremost he would try to be the servant of Christian awareness in the diocese of Crateús. The

Christian community of Crateús, moved and animated by its faith, would construct all the buildings necessary for the welfare of the city.

I recall the three residents of Crateús who offered two *quadras* of land [approx. 8.5 acres] for a minor seminary. Many men of Ceará now in high positions had passed through the school of discipline and seriousness called minor seminary. I had been vice-rector of the minor and major seminary of the archdiocese of João Pessoa for seven years, and a teacher there for fourteen. I had seen hundreds of boys enter the minor seminary. In recent years only three to five percent of them reached the priesthood.

What a huge investment in property, equipment, teachers, and maintenance, and with what disappointing results!

How could I have justified a minor seminary in the diocese of Crateús, where there were so few priests and so little money? I had to reject the proposal.

Clearly, we had come to a crossroads. It was a risky position to take. In the first place, I was frustrating expectations about the new bishop. In the second place, I was taking a position before listening to the clergy and laity, and seeing whether or not this was everybody's thinking. Not being a diplomat, I thought only of being consistent with my conscience when I voiced my opinions.

Would it have been better to wait, and get to know the people first?

It is not my intention in this testimonial to make value judgments on the various options I have made. Others would have made other options, perhaps a great deal more valid than my own. I have no wish to pass judgment on those options. I seek only to recount, in all honesty, what I have lived and experienced myself.

I recall that, after the welcoming ceremonies in front of the cathedral, we headed for the bishop's palace. This was another thing that made a big impression on me. Even in a small, poor town I would have expected the bishop to have a fine house, yes. But not one of the fanciest houses in town! The bishop's palace had been built, lovingly and affectionately, by Father José Maria Moreira do Bonfim, a pastor in Crateús for so many years, in expectation of the new bishop's arrival. Everyone had chipped in, from the Fourth Engineers to the very poorest of the poor. There were persons who could only give an egg. The widow's mite!

The bishop was awaited with fondness and affection, and his residence was called the bishop's palace. On my arrival, I asked that it be called simply the bishop's house, so that it could be something more simple—at least in intention. I would perhaps be unable to make it "everyone's house"—the house of a brother, not a potentate—but at least the name "bishop's house" would be a challenge to my conscience.

When we arrived at the residence, Governor Virgílio Távora called me aside. "You see," he told me, "I've signed agreements with the archdiocese, and the other dioceses of Ceará—now I can offer you the chance to sign agreements on behalf of your new diocese."

"Governor," I replied, "I abide by what I have just said. I shall sign no agreement with the government. Because I shall not be putting up new buildings here. My work is mainly as an educator of consciences, in the light of faith—so that the Christian community may take the necessary services in hand along with everyone else. The community may sign agreements if it wishes, but not the bishop or the priests."

I think that that was quite an important position to take.

I remember, too, a reception given me in the bishop's residence. The invitees were from the middle class, with very few poor—very few from slum neighborhoods.

Obviously I could not but be most grateful for any gesture of kindness and friendship. And I thanked my guests from my heart. But I let it be known that I would have been happier if the lowly, and the very poorest, had been there.

Father Bonfim, gallant and friendly, now arranged still another reception, this time in what was then called the Crateús Club. And invited persons from the barrios of the city. It was a very nice gesture of friendship on his part.

Earlier, when I was still in the diocese of São Luís do Maranhão, as bishop-elect of Crateús, I received a letter from a well-informed resident of Crateús, which read, in part:

Here in Crateús great expectations surround the arrival of the new bishop. I have the pleasure of informing Your Excellency that the minister of transportation, Expedito Machado, who is from Crateús, wants to give the diocese a radio station—

Crateús Educational Radio, it will be called. We only await
Your Excellency's arrival.

And it was true. Later, after the fall of João Goulart, Expedito
Machado left the country. I met him and his wife in Rome during
the Second Vatican Council, and he told me, "I want to set up a
Pedro Machado Foundation in Crateús, and give you an educational radio station."

My answer was the same. I repeated what I had told the people,
and Dr. Salim, the day I had arrived. The bishop of Crateús would
not be a "builder of civilization." I did not consider this my
mission. Mine would be a discreet mission of service to the people
of Crateús, to help the people take up the reins of destiny in its own
country. If the community wanted a radio station and this would be
of service to the people, that would be fine.

"Five years from now," replied the former minister, "you'll be
sorry."

This was in 1964. Five years later the diocese was forbidden
access to educational radio, and the interdict lasted eleven years! I
was absolutely forbidden to speak over the radio at all—in a
diocese where virtually everyone was Catholic, and where this was
the bishop's means of communication with the isolated interior,
and where the radio is on all day long in every house with a
transistor.

In issuing the prohibition, the director of radio communications
said that it came from higher up. But he declined to reveal the
source. A formal request addressed to the regional delegate of the
pertinent branch of government went without a reply. A friend told
me that he has seen a written order from the federal police. I cannot
confirm that this was the source.

Only in 1980 was the diocese once more given time on educational radio.

But the *pastoral* reasons for which I had refused ownership of a
radio station were solid, I think, and I was not "sorry." And today I
am still doing what I intended to do back then.

3

TAKING SIDES WITH THE POOR
AND OPPRESSED

Every day my eyes rove over the diocese of Crateús. My ears hear the voice of this people of the rain forest. My heart throbs and suffers with the daily struggle of the *camponeses.*

It is very hard to see this part of the world correctly without passing by way of the life and struggle of the people of the countryside.

The inhabitants of Crateús have a human face, a face bronzed by the blazing sun, the hospitable face of a brother and sister.

The diocese has a population of 350,000, in an area of 22,000 square kilometers. Some 88 percent of the population is strictly rural, and the remaining 12 percent depends heavily on the local economy, migration, and good seasons in the fields.

Produce is predominantly maize, common beans, manioc, cotton, and castor beans. Local prices for these crops fluctuate, but they never cover production costs.

Example: in November 1978 a farmer could sell a sack of beans for 600 cruzeiros. With this amount he could buy a hundred cans of cooking oil, a sack of rice, a sack of sugar, and four kilos of coffee. But in April of the following year, right after the harvest, the same sack of beans brought only 230 cruzeiros. No more oil, sugar, or rice. (Not even the four kilos of coffee, which now cost 240 cruzeiros!).

No social class but the people of the bush would have the stamina to withstand this great a pressure on their basic budget.

All manufactured goods, which come here from the large cities, are sold for wildly and progressively inflated prices. Each year the buying power of a worker's wages or salary plummets. And so the youth migrate to the big commercial centers—Rio, São Paulo, Brasília—and Amazônia. They have no education, and so they take the lowest-paying, most insecure jobs. They all have sentimental hearts, so they get homesick and come back. Now it is all but impossible for them to readapt to the suicidal life of a farmer. And they become nomads, with serious consequences for their families and their economic status.

Sons of better-off families go away to college in the big cities. Once they have their degrees, they don't come back. Their place of origin fails to offer them a market for professional work that promises any advancement. And this concentration of "technological brains" in far-off urban centers drains the countryside of its intellectual elite. The poor enrich the rich.

The land is unjustly distributed. Some 12 percent of landowners control 62 percent of the land, whereas half of the active population of the countryside has no land to work.

No credit is extended to the small farmer or the landless worker. Both continue in total dependence, with no way out, even over the long term. Official projects favor the big commercial farms. The best that the small farmers and the landless can hope for is a lease.

Public opinion is almost always indifferent to the scandal of this genocide.

The church of Crateús seeks to nourish its faith at the wellspring of the gospel. Its faith teaches us the following:

• The face of this bush people conceals, and reveals, the face of God.
• You can't love and serve the living God without loving and serving this people.
• This people is the human image of a creative God, and is called to create its own history.
• Our God chooses the lowly, the weak, the oppressed, and the poor to confound the wise and mighty.
• United, this people is Yahweh's friend and mediation. Through this people Yahweh is to bring down the mighty from their thrones,

send the rich away empty-handed, and set captives free.
• Any society concentrating economic, political, and cultural power in the hands of elites, marginalizing the masses of the people, is rotten, unChristian, and suicidal.

Inspired with this vision of faith and this hope, the church of Crateús intends to make an option for the lowly and the weak, an option for the people of the bush.

4

VISITING THE CLERGY

One of my first decisions on arriving in the diocese was to go out to meet the priests as a *brother*, not as "the bishop." I did not want to visit them as the head of the diocese, invested with canonical powers, and owed the obedience of his priests. I wanted to go to them as a brother and friend. I wanted to listen to the clergy. I had "parachuted" into their midst. I had no knowledge of the context in which I was going to be living, and no pastoral experience in that region. They had the merit of a devoted life in this hinterland, *sertão,* of Ceará. Theirs was the merit of having been, and continuing to be, the local church. It was my moral duty to listen to them.

I went to all ten of my parishes the very month I arrived. I always asked that no reception be held for me. I came not as the bishop, but as a visiting brother. And so I was able to converse with each of them in all simplicity.

I found a good clergy, one bearing the mark of a solid priestly formation. They had received their training from Bishop José Tupinambá da Frota and the Lazarist Fathers of the seminary in Fortaleza. I wish to express my profound gratitude for the excellent contribution made by Dom José and the seminary personnel who had molded generations of priests.

Now, did the priests expect what the civil leaders and authorities had expected?

In my initial conversation with each of the priests I inquired into the pastoral ministry—catechetics, liturgy, and the religious practices of the masses of the people at the chapels and main churches. I asked whether there was any specialized "Catholic action," and I asked what each priest expected of the bishop.

Inasmuch as I did not pose the explicit question, whether their expectations were the same as those of the civil authorities, I have no proof that it was. But today, from what was the practice then, I conclude that this may well have been the case. For example, there were priests running a high school. There were priests building schools and hiring teachers. There were priests starting new projects with help from outside. There was some effort to imitate the former bishop, but not much. The resources of the eight scattered parishes that had belonged to the diocese of Sobral were limited.

In many dioceses, priests establishing social projects were rewarded with the title of monsignor or canon.

As I say, I asked whether there was any specialized "Catholic action." Every priest said no. I myself had just come from ten years as regional assistant for the Jocists—Catholic Worker Youth—in Nordeste. In São Luís do Maranhão, over the course of six years, and with the blessing of my old friend Archbishop José de Medeiros Delgado, I had managed to set up the Jocists, Workers' Catholic Action, and Catholic Rural Youth. I had hoped to find something, at least, in the new diocese.

But I want to give due credit to the work of the Crateús priests, their apostolic zeal in visiting their far-flung chapels, their long journeys on horseback over nearly impossible trails, their zeal for religious education, and their interest in their social works, which they considered to be in line with their ministry as priests and a service to the community.

I want to emphasize my praise for these priests. I have no wish to underestimate in any way anything that I found them doing, although *my* "model of church" did not include this sort of "social ministry" by "builders of civilization."

5

TOWARD A TRADE UNION

Back in Crateús after my visitation of the ten parishes, I went on the local radio. My message was essentially this: The diocese of Crateús was predominantly rural. A bare 12 percent of the population lived in towns; 88 percent lived in the country. And those who lived in town depended on farm life for many things. More than half of the active population of the countryside was landless. In the district of Parambu 90 percent of the adults living in the country were illiterate.

In a situation like this, I said, I felt I had to suggest that citizens avail themselves of the law of the land. The law said that citizens had the right to organize in trade unions. Inasmuch as the most representative category among the people of my diocese was that of the rural poor—landless or small landowners—I was going to try to give them an opportunity to become familiar with trade unionism. They ought to know the labor laws, I said, so as to be able to form independent unions.

And I announced on this broadcast that I intended to form a team that would visit them in their homes, in order to familiarize them, in their own context, with the law, the structure of a union, and the ABCs of union operation. Then they could form their own association, which could then apply for recognition by the Ministry of Labor as a rural workers' union.

When I got home from the radio station I found a friend—a businessman and landowner, and member of quite a well-to-do family—waiting for me. "I've been listening to you on the radio," he said. "Tell me, if we have to put the workers off the land because of union agitation, do you have other land to offer them?"

So I had the impression that I had touched the second sore spot of the Crateús elite. The first had been that they expected me to be a "builder of civilization." The second, now, was that they expected me to take an interest in the middle class, as others did, rather than in the lowly. And so what I was doing looked like agitation. It looked as if I were disturbing the peace!

Again during the course of those first days and weeks, I was invited to dinner by the Lions' Club. An officer welcomed me in the name of his fellow members. He stated that it was a joy to them all to be able to offer their bishop this sign of friendship. In token of their friendship and cooperation, they would put on a fund-raiser, with an airline trip to São Paulo and back as the prize. All the proceeds would go to diocesan social works.

Moved, I thanked the Lions for this gesture of friendship. But it was my duty in conscience, I said, to be honest with them. My first and foremost "social work," I told them, would be the conscientization of the people of the countryside, so long marginalized in the social process. And secondly, I would help them do what the law said they had the right to do: organize rural workers' unions.

"Rural unions?" the officer cried. "That's subversive!"

And so I realized that my project for society did not coincide with that of the Crateús elite. Clearly, our outlooks and aims were incompatible. There was going to be tension and conflict.

6

RELIGIOUS EDUCATION
WORKSHOPS

At the time—August and September 1964—I did not fully understand the mentality underlying the various projects of the Crateús elite. I did, however, perceive very clearly that they did not coincide with the projects that, in my view, ought to be undertaken by the pastoral workers of the diocesan church. They did not coincide; they were incompatible.

Purely hypothetically, if I had had more diplomatic tact, if I had been more of a political person, perhaps I would not have provoked this sense of incompatibility so soon—right from the start. Perhaps I could have created the illusion that our projects coincided. But to create this illusion would have been dishonesty on my part.

In that first year I thought: I have a dream, a vision of society, an ideal that the church ought to be involved in implementing. But I am entirely against any form of clericalism in the proposal of undertakings for society. The church should be the gospel leaven in any societal undertaking.

Meanwhile I realized that I did not have to start from scratch. Bishop Motta of the diocese of Sobral, which had included eight of the parishes of the new diocese of Crateús, was a persevering advocate of religious education. Father Manuel Edmilson Cruz held catechetics seminars, or workshops. And the Better World Movement promoted pastoral planning.

I consulted my priests, and we decided to have a religious education workshop in every parish, once a year, from 1965 to 1967.

The workshops were geared to married couples. It was my conviction that parents are their children's first religious educators in God's intention, and therefore irreplaceable. Teachers, educators, catechists, and the whole Christian people were invited.

They were lively, active workshops. I discovered that the diocese had hundreds of humble, unknown catechists, all proclaiming the gospel with their own individual knack and resources.

I was profoundly happy to make this discovery, and I began to see the course that my work and my responsibility should take. The priests and I agreed to give these "amateur catechists" better training. They were looking for encouragement and advice, and we had no program to provide it with zeal and competency.

Of these initiatives was born the Diocesan Department of Religious Education, which has encouraged and inspired the pastoral work of religious education for years now. Through direct visits, meetings for study and evaluation, and, up until 1969, a weekly program on Crateús Educational Radio, this department spurred religious education throughout the diocese.

We distributed the following set of objectives and guidelines to the parishes:

PARISH RELIGIOUS EDUCATION WORKSHOPS

Objectives

The 1965 Pastoral Action Plan for the diocese of Crateús provides for a series of three religious education workshops:
1965: The Good News of God's Kingdom for All
1966: The Bible and Religious Education
1967: Liturgy and Religious Education
1. Before setting up any religious education program in a parish or diocese, those in charge should be aware of the dignity and importance of religious education, and of our Christian responsibility in its regard. The 1965, 1966, and 1967 Religious Education Workshops are designed to further this "catechetical conscientization."
2. The Religious Education Workshops for 1966 have the

purpose of placing the Christians of the diocese in the presence of the word of God in the Bible—a word to be carried in everyone's heart and lived by all, in community.

Guidelines for the Parish Religious Education Workshops

The pastor, as the one in charge of the Religious Education workshop, along with those entrusted with the task of religious education in the parish, should give timely notice of a meeting of the personnel who will be conducting the workshop. This meeting should be used to present a general overview of the workshop, then to set up the committees that will be needed for its successful operation.

The pastor should serve as general coordinator. In addition, each committee will select, from among its members, a chairperson who will be responsible for the guidance and supervision of the activities of that committee.

Each committee should divide its assignments appropriately among its members. For example, the presentation committee should select, for each subject to be presented, someone whose personal aptitudes and abilities would make him or her the right choice to present that subject.

Each committee should meet as often as will be necessary to carry out its duties in a fitting manner. The pastor, being responsible for the general supervision of the workshop, should take part in all committee meetings.

7

DIOCESAN CARITAS

I gradually came to an appreciation of the extreme poverty prevailing in the diocese, and the challenge that it presented for the pastoral ministry. Most of the *camponeses* had no land. Small landholders were unable to live from what they produced. Profits were intercepted by commercial intermediaries. The majority of the population of the countryside and the outskirts of the cities lived in disgraceful ignorance. Our pastoral ministry simply could not remain aloof from this deplorable situation.

And so I decided to initiate some very modest social action. We began with Caritas Católica, toward the end of 1964 and the beginning of 1965.

The diocesan Caritas offices were affiliated with national Caritas, receiving commodities from the United States and trying to distribute them in accordance with pedagogical criteria of community development.

These commodities consisted of surplus farm products. Putting them on the market in the United States would inevitably have provoked lower prices there, and a consequent crisis for farmers. Disposing of them at sea, or burning them, would have caused an international scandal. So the United States "used its head" and decided to send them as a gift to the countries of the Third World. At the average of every three minutes, a boat would leave the United States for some one of seventy-two countries, carrying its farm surplus cargo. On every box or can was printed, "Gift of the People of the United States of America."

In this way the United States managed to create a kind and generous image of itself, kept its farm prices up, and continued to maintain and reinforce the mechanisms of the concentration of raw materials, technologies, and centers of economic and political decision-making in its own hands. The more "conscientized" among our people would say, "They give with one hand and take with two."

We on the receiving end had become accustomed to holding out our hands like beggars. We were coming from a background of more than four hundred years of dependency. We were inclined to forget that "persons grow when they give, not when they receive."

For three or four years, we made use of Caritas Católica as a tool in community activity and in the collective experiences of our farmers. The commodities distributed were a spur and motivation for community plantations, team farming, the building of small social centers and schools, and a more general participation by the community in all community affairs.

This community action did the people of the countryside a great deal of good, as far as I was able to ascertain. And so I have to acknowledge the merit of Caritas Católica. It opened a door. It was an intermediate step on a long journey.

But in 1968 we met, drew up a balance sheet of receipts and distribution of commodities, and came to the conclusion that we were helping the United States more than we were helping ourselves.

And so we decided to stop. This meant that we would suddenly be left without a Caritas office, without the transportation network that had been developed, and without the seven persons who worked full-time in those operations. For a year, then, we paid a scanty stipend to two persons who undertook to attend the communities that had been assisted by Caritas. We had no further resources.

Today, at a little distance, this seems to me to have been a sound intuition, based on a serious analysis of our experience.

8

OUR GRASSROOTS EDUCATION MOVEMENT

Wouldn't it have been better to continue to maintain the Caritas office and keep helping the communities?

We all have a little of the child in us. And a child always needs "candy"—always needs an enticement. The commodities we received through Caritas were like candy—an enticement to participate in a community undertaking.

But we found that many persons failed to bind themselves to the community as such, to community life for its own value. The main thing was the commodities, the hand-outs. When these failed, many would abandon the community, and the community would be in crisis.

This was our first effort at this kind of social action. It was very modest at first. But it was realistic, it seems to me, seeing that our region had never been served by organized, critical social action.

So now we returned to our grassroots education. This was in 1965. It seemed to me that base-level education was indispensable if we wanted to engage in human promotion and the development of the people. Pope Paul VI, in his letter *Populorum Progressio,* had stated that no program of genuine development was possible without effective base-level education.

In Brazil, the best-known tool for grassroots education was the MEB—the *Movimento de Educação de Base,* Basic Education Movement. The MEB had resulted from an agreement between the federal government and the CNBB *(Conferência Nacional dos Bispos do Brasil),* the National Conference of the Bishops of Brazil. The government provided the financing, and the bishops assumed responsibility for the organization of educational radio broadcasts, the training of monitors, and other educational activities.

The program itself was entrusted to the laity. The bishops retained only national supervision and the presidency of each diocesan system.

The MEB—which is not all that there is to base-level education in Brazil—was born, to my way of thinking, under the sign of clericalism. Grassroots education should be a service to the entire secular community, and should not per se have any confessional ties. I opposed the bishops' role at the national level, and in the presidency of the local systems, from the very beginning. But that was the way the MEB was, by statute and by agreement. The diocese had no resources for the financing of an independent program of this sort. And so I was obliged to sign the agreement by which I would be president of the local MEB.

In Crateús, the MEB took over the community action that Caritas had begun, and carried it on with a somewhat better developed methodology.

Was it necessary for the CNBB to assume the national direction and local presidency of the MEB in order to support base-level education?

When the church has pastoral reasons for furthering community services that do not specifically pertain to its mission and its ministry, it does so by way of "supplement," or stopgap. It would have been better for the church to entrust the administration of the MEB entirely to the laity, and simply take up the defense of their just hopes for the movement. It is more in the spirit of the gospel simply to support and defend a base-level educational movement, which is not that of the church, and is not a direct execution of its mission of service to the people.

Then one day we simply had to close the MEB in the diocese of Crateús. Among the seven persons working full-time in the local system was an Italian social worker by the name of Maria Teresa Nodari. I received a telegram from the bishop who was the president of the national MEB directive council, advising us of Maria Teresa's summary dismissal. The local bishop, statutory president of the diocesan system, had not been consulted. Neither had Maria Teresa, an adult, responsible person, well-suited to her position.

To me, this was a clear contradiction of the very meaning of grassroots education. It meant that base-level education was a sham. And so I protested to my brother bishop who had given the order. He held firm, however, and so, in the absence of reasons to justify the dismissal, we decided to close the MEB.

This meant that we would once more be without the persons who had been working with us, this time in the MEB. We had no resources to maintain the system ourselves, what with the needed transport facilities and the seven full-time jobs involved.

I think that consistency with our own conscience, our own vision, pursuit of the human and social undertakings we have committed ourselves to, will sometimes lead to painful decisions.

This had been our second attempt at social action. It was an attempt to set up the conditions under which the communities of the countryside could become analytically aware of the real situation in which they were living, and could organize, militantly, for a process of social change.

None of this was very clear to us as yet. But a kind of "twilight intuition" gave a certain orientation to our options.

9

EDUCATION FOR THE UNION MOVEMENT

In the area of social action, besides Caritas Católica and base-level education, we attributed great importance to education in the concepts and function of the trade union. We knew that the union movement ought to have total autonomy. The persons involved—members of the various trades and professions—ought to be independent in their quest for organization and in their demands for the rights of the working class.

Rural unions, even in the good years, 1964 and 1965, were looked on with a great deal of mistrust. In our situation in the diocese, it was middle-class preconceptions that were particularly prejudicial to union work. We had had a military coup, a so-called revolution, and unionism was in considerable trouble. It seemed right to us to offer it some breathing space, where the *camponeses* could learn labor legislation and the structure and organization of a union. Then they would be able to form their own trade associations, which would subsequently receive official recognition from the Ministry of Labor.

And so we invited a French union organizer, Ms. Paulette Ripert, to set up a team. Paulette had been a militant member of the French Confederation of Christian Workers for ten years, and came with the recommendation of saintly Archbishop de Provenchères of Aix-en-Provence.

After a great deal of patient, generous, and misunderstood work by Paulette, we finally had the joy of seeing five unions, in five of the ten townships of our diocese, recognized by the Labor Ministry. Then in 1969 Paulette had a serious accident and had to spend a long time in Fortaleza recuperating. By the time she was well, repression had grown to the point where she could no longer stay in Brazil.

Was our union activity the same as what eventually came to be called "union opposition"?

The expression was unknown at the time, and was coined only several years later. But if we compare our education in unionism with the substance of what is proposed today by "union opposition," we do find some affinity. We rejected the official union blueprint. We refused to be tied to the Labor Ministry. We rejected any interference by government, employers, or politicians in our internal affairs. The church refused to organize unions or run them. Our work was education in unionism, as a stopgap measure, in order to assist the *camponeses* to organize their own completely autonomous unions.

In the course of her work of education in unionism, which took her from house to house in the villages and districts of the diocese, Paulette discovered that the wives of rural workers lacked their husbands' level of conscientization, their husbands' opportunities. Male rural workers belonged to the unions, analyzed their problems, became familiar with the law, and acquired a certain professional awareness, whereas the women participated in nothing, continued to be dependent, and were lacking in any critical consciousness of their situation.

And so a little movement was launched in the diocese called "Women's Promotion." It started with small things—women meeting in groups in a few parts of the diocese to discuss their problems, to become critically aware of them, and to feel the call to join the unions themselves in order to defend the cause of the field workers in general and the cause of women's interests in particular.

Because it was not yet on a secure footing, when Paulette left the movement collapsed.

10

A CONTRACT WITH THE
INTER-AMERICAN FOUNDATION

We felt the need to keep up the work of human promotion and grassroots education in another form.

In 1973 I signed an agreement with FINA, *Fundação Interamericana,* the Inter-American Foundation. For three years FINA would supplement the financial support of a diocesan community promotion project.

Seven persons with intermediate or higher training were involved in this project, and their sphere of activity ranged from the Crateús barrios to the communities in the bush. Their main concern was to get adults to take an interest in the process of their own education.

After three years of work, the diocese as such drew up a balance sheet, for the purpose of critiquing the pedagogical effectiveness of the project and international intervention in it, especially on the part of the United States. We decided not to renew the agreement, even though the Inter-American Foundation was ready to do so.

Why did the diocese agree to a project financed with American money?

Few if any of our actions are chemically pure in their motivation. They are mixed. However, we saw something a little different about FINA.

With Caritas Católica what we received was surplus farm produce from the United States, a "gift of the American People."

Accepting this aid meant creating a kindly image of the United States, but new dependencies for us, besides our being used as a way to maintain the farm economy of an exploitative nation.

With the Inter-American Foundation, despite the irrefutable ambiguity of the arrangement, there was a positive facet. The United States Senate had given its stamp of approval to an agency whose president was a Protestant minister with broad experience among the poverty-stricken populations of Asia, and whose basic philosophy incorporated a pedagogy that respected the participation of the people. In Latin America FINA employed some fifty full-time specialists and fostered projects involving a fair measure of popular participation. In fact its sponsorship of these projects was conditioned on popular participation.

I discussed all this with FINA officials at great length, both in Crateús and in Washington. I wanted to know if there would be any financial pressure applied to our ideologies, our internal options, our pedagogy.

I was formally guaranteed that there would be no interference of any kind. There had been accusations against the foundation from various sources, from the intellectual community in Brazil and abroad, for whatever comes from the United States is automatically granted subservient to the process of domination and imperialism.

I knew of no cooperative agencies that were totally pure. I knew of no agencies altogether free from the taint of imperialism. And I had the explicit guarantee of the Inter-American Foundation that there would be no interference with our pedagogical options, our own internal processes. And so I signed a three-year agreement.

11

THE ROAD TO AN INTERCONTINENTAL "ECUMENISM" OF LIBERATION

TAKING ON CHALLENGES

Here I take the liberty of transcribing parts of an article I wrote for the German press in 1979:

My life has been marked by a certain poem of Rabindranath Tagore. It is the story of a generous prince, who has gone on a long journey. A beggar spies his carriage from a distance and thinks, "This prince is surely generous. I shall beg an alms of him." The prince draws near, and the beggar extends his hand. "Alms for the love of God!" he cries.

The prince commands the driver to halt, and alights. He embraces the beggar. "Friend," he asks, "what do you have in the sack on your back?"

"Wheat," replies the other.

"Will you give me a little of your wheat?"

The beggar gives the prince some of his wheat.

Much moved, the prince thanks the beggar and makes off. The beggar, astonished and frightened, returns to his hovel. And when he opens his sack, he sees that the wheat has all been changed to gold.

Moral: It is more blessed to give than to receive.

Humanity's Southern peoples will be blessed by liberation when they give of themselves.

If the Germans had been a peripheral, dependent people, and had not accumulated a mature cultural experience, would the Marshall Plan have brought them economic liberation?

The peoples of the southern hemisphere have a centuries-long history of colonial or capitalistic dependency. Can aid from the peoples of the North do anything but prolong their reflexes and habits of dependency?

The lame and the crippled who have accustomed themselves to going about on crutches find it more and more difficult to walk on their own two feet. And so they continue to use the crutches.

In my own faith perspective, God makes the Southern peoples, like those of the North, to the divine image and likeness, and this means they are to be *creators, like God.* By exercising their creative power, they will find the road to freedom.

The law of least effort is applicable here. When we find plenty of help, we generally refuse hard, painful creative effort.

Alienation is a mental disease. We have heard for so long and so often how poor, illiterate, and incapable we are, that we interiorize the certitude that the solution to our problems can only come from without. You don't build a participatory project for a society with alienated men and women. We must experience our own creative autonomy in an economic and political practice on our own level.

THE STRATEGY OF UNILATERAL RELATIONSHIPS

For decades now, the rich countries have been offering us unilateral assistance. Moved by their Christian heritage, perhaps, they have thought, "Those with bread should share with those lacking it." And they have added, "We have money, technology, know-how, and missionaries. Let's send them to the poor countries—missionaries, experts, money, and all."

Through assistance, governmental and nongovernmental, through the organisms of the churches, the poor nations have received a great deal.

I am not speaking of "assistance" with strings attached, which is simply a ravenous form of exploitation, as if we were children willing to be bribed with "candy" our whole lives long.

I am speaking of well-intentioned assistance born of generosity. How often has the official message of the churches spurred and encouraged this sort of help!

The experience of the step to bilaterality in our relationships with the rich nations has itself been rich.

Many aid agencies have discovered that the root of the impoverishment of the southern hemisphere is in the northern hemisphere. Rather than "assisting," one should awaken in the "underdeveloped" countries an awareness of the ongoing mechanisms of exploitation. If a sophisticated capitalism feeds on the exploitation of peripheral, dependent capitalisms, then its "assistance" is a lie and an insult, for it coexists with the structures, and legitimating ideologies, of dependency.

A radical critical awareness emerges only from within a transforming practice. The practice of the radical change of the structures and ideologies of domination will mean the death of the Trilateral Agreement, the power-idol, the oligarchical control of the means of production, technologies, communications media, knowledge, and political decisions.

These contradictions can be a challenge to even the best-intentioned among us. We interiorize the "certitude" of our incapacity to radically transform prevailing structures. And we run off in search of unilateral assistance, labeling it "friendly cooperation" when it is really condescending interference, and not a legitimate substitute for an "assisted" people's own efforts.

I am not speaking of intentions that so often are generous and sincere. Nor am I speaking of the witness of so many missionaries and other dedicated persons. I admire this witness profoundly.

I am not a "voluntarist." I believe that permanent structures of domination and exploitation render subjective intentionality ineffective.

THE STRATEGY OF MULTILATERAL RELATIONSHIPS

For me, then, genuine brotherly and sisterly cooperation is *mutual* assistance.

Unilateral assistance starts with a false premise: "The North has, the South has not." But today it is sufficiently clear that the North has *and* the South has. It is only that we "have" in different ways. But these ways are valid and complementary.

The North has its cultural universe, its economic universe, its political, religious, technological, and symbolic universes. The contribution of the North is irreplaceable. Without it, there is no building a free tomorrow for humanity.

Those who live in the North need not succumb to an inferiority complex. They have the high dignity and worth of belonging to their wonderful universe. But let them radically eschew any superiority complex!

The South, too, has its cultural universe, and its economic, political, religious, technological, and symbolic universes. Without the irreplaceable contribution of the South, there is no building a free tomorrow for humanity.

We of the South must tear out by the roots the inferiority complex instilled in us by centuries of colonialism and neocolonialism. We have the high dignity and worth of being the southern hemisphere of humanity! Let us reject any kind of nostalgia for colonial times, any kind of humiliating, abasing dependency.

Inasmuch as North and South, differently but in complementarity, "have"—then it is no longer *unilateral assistance* that is in order—no longer a matter of the *North sharing* with the South.

It is a matter of *sharing together,* of harmonizing our comradely cooperation. Any kind of unilateral decision-making is merely a prolongation of the old scheme of relationships.

I call my conceptualization a "multilateral strategy."

I believe that this is the new challenge facing our awareness and our conscience.

But this slow, gradual implantation of *socialization*—in theological language, of *communion*—supposes and demands a breach with prevailing structures and ideologies of domination and dependency.

A struggle for justice on the part of the oppressed is essential. There is a creative sharing to be accepted here, too. We cannot hope that the *North will be radically converted and bestow on the oppressed* the lovely present of justice for all!

The power-idol must topple from its throne, with empty hands, through the efficacious intermediary of the Angel of Yahweh—the little ones of the earth, united, organized.

Here, the gospel is irreplaceable for the conscientization of the oppressed in their struggle for liberation.

IMPLANTATION OF THE NEW STRATEGY

How could these diverse, complementary contributions of North and South ever be harmonized, without mutual acknowledgment in understanding and in love?

I think that there is a crucial priority to be observed here. And that is the mutual discovery by North and South of the *human face of the other hemisphere.*

What can the North do to discover the human face of the South? What can the North do to reveal its human face to its sisters and brothers of the South?

What can the South do to discover the human face of the North? What can the South do to reveal its human face to its brothers and sisters of the North?

No one is in a position to lay out a fully developed strategy. Any apriorism is to be rejected out of hand. North and South must undertake a multilateral practice, starting with those who feel themselves called to be the agents of this practice.

Let us initiate a practice of multilateral relationships. Searching together, in humility, *we shall encounter one another!*

12

LITURGICAL MINISTRY

Along so many hesitant paths, little by little we are readying a new type of project for a church—a church that will be the leaven of encouragement and strength for the whole life of the whole community.

And we have not forgotten the liturgy, where the faithful come together to celebrate their life, their faith, and the liberation of which they dream.

And so I asked one of the priests to go to the Institute of Liturgical Ministry in Medellín, run by the Latin American Bishops' Conference, and take a course. And I asked a young woman to take a course at the National Institute of Liturgical Ministry in Rio.

Through no fault of theirs, neither was ever able to have any influence on liturgical creativity in the diocese of Crateús. We have to admit that the diocese failed to make much progress in liturgical creativity and expression. This is something we have to look at and attend to in our journey to the future.

We hesitate, we vacillate, between the official liturgy, that vessel of such great wealth of centuries past—and we must not neglect this wealth—but heavily stereotyped, centralized, and strongly concerned with theological orthodoxy, and, on the other hand, the popular liturgy, with its religious, symbolic, and affective universe almost completely unknown to theologians, pastors, and intellectuals, and with its undeniable ambiguities.

We are looking for a liturgical expression with a language,

gestures, and symbols that will welcome, and reveal, the people's pilgrimage in its struggle for liberation. We reject "immobilism," and legalistic rigidity, but we have not yet found a way to incorporate popular culture, and the liberation process, into the liturgy.

I hope that a diocesan church with the face of the people will give the church universal a popular liturgy in strict fidelity to the gospel.

13

BASE-LEVEL CHURCH COMMUNITIES

I had heard of the CEBs, *comunidades eclesiais de base,* the base-level or grassroots church communities, from the start. I had read books about them, like those of Father José Marins and Father Raimundo Caramuru.

This was a utopian project, and I loved it. What enthusiasm! But these were books, and their proposals had not been tested by practice. They included no verification of their practical pedagogical merits, their actual effectiveness in pastoral practice.

It was a call, as any challenging utopia is, for incarnation, for experimentation, for implementation.

And so we began, step by step. Caritas Católica helped get the communities going by distributing commodities. Paulo Freire's "pedagogy of the oppressed," which we tried to apply in Crateús in 1967 and 1968, in forty "enlightenment circles," helped us build our project up from a starting point among the people and the basic realities of the life of the people. I visited other parts of the country, where pastoral experimentation with base communities was already being conducted.

In my view, the base communities afforded a fine "basic space," where the people of the countryside and the outskirts of the cities could engage in the practice of freedom, political practice.

The people was marginalized when it came to the national political scene. The national security doctrine, the very foundation of the Brazilian regime, denied that the nation was the people. The people didn't count. The nation was the power elite, and the people simply had to await their redemption by the power elite.

And so we had no expectations of anything from the national political community. Educators like Paulo Freire were brutally shunned for proposing popular participation in political life. All expressions of popular culture were suspect. And so we had nowhere else to go. The church had to assume the responsibility of offering the people a basic space where it could exercise liberative practice—the practice of freedom—and political practice.

The base communities began especially as space for human promotion. What we were aiming at was social action. The bishops of the northeast had decided that human promotion should have priority in pastoral work.

For the people, however, human promotion was not the main thing. The main thing was God's word. God is the living, vital, permanent reference point in the people's heart. Little by little the celebration of the word of the Lord, and the Lord's day, took priority.

Our intention was that the base communities would be the church at the grassroots, a space or place for popular participation, in which the people of the countryside—the lowly, the poor, the weak, the oppressed—might grow to become the agent of its own progress, the protagonist of its own history.

This was the beautiful, utopian ideal that filled the hearts of the people, and I spoke of it in our meetings and discussions time and again.

14

TENTH ANNIVERSARY

In 1974, the diocese of Crateús was ten years old. But I decided not to have a celebration. I wanted to avoid anything like triumphalism on that occasion.

I invited the entire diocese to draw up a balance sheet of our ten-year journey together. And we discovered something that, for me, came as a shock, and in large measure determined the direction of later work.

I had spoken with such enthusiasm of "the people as the agent of its own progress," as "protagonist of its own history." I had condemned "colonialist and neocolonialist interference" in all their forms. I had claimed that the church had been the "tool of colonizers" in the days of discovery and evangelization.

What I now discovered was that I had been doing the same thing all over again in Crateús!

True, I had paid a great deal of attention to the CEBs. But take our diocesan assemblies. Every year we held an all-diocesan meeting. Some one hundred representatives from our ten parishes would be in attendance. For a whole week, we would conduct an evaluation of our work. We would invite a knowledgeable theologian to advise us in our theological reflection, and we would work out directives for the use of the parishes in setting up their pastoral plans. I had fallen victim to authoritarian centralism—with nicer names, of course, and I had committed it only unconsciously or semiconsciously—but there it was.

This was an enormous shock for me on our tenth anniversary. Radical measures had to be taken. In the diocesan pastoral process, *voz e vez*—"voice and vote"—would have to be restored to the CEBs. We would hold no more diocesan assemblies for the purpose of overall planning, or for the elaboration of directives to be incorporated into all the different parish plans. I asked each tiny community to gather in its own locale, draw up an accounting of its pastoral practice in the year just past, and propose its own pastoral plan for the year to come.

The pastoral teams of each parish took these plans, just as they came from the little communities, read them, and were helped to discover the objectives of these communities and the routes they had selected to attain them. When any of this was not clear, the plan would be returned to the base community that had drawn it up with the question, "What do you want to say? What do you have in view?" And the community would have to make its proposal more explicit. But it was not a matter of having it *corrected* by the parish team.

Then the parish team would try to discern the underlying expectations of the plans. What did this particular little CEB expect of the parish team? These hopes were often unexpressed. But they were there. Finally, with these expectations before them, the parish team would develop a response, in the form of its own program for educational support.

And so the pyramid had been turned upside down. Now the planning was done basically at the grass roots. And the ones to do the listening—the ones to be at the service of the others, for the development of each parish's respective plan—were the parish team.

Now the ten parish teams brought their programs for educational support to the Diocesan Pastoral Council. The council would read and reflect on each one, seek to identify its implicit expectations, and work out a—still very imperfect—general educational program.

Of course, the process as I present it here is a little idealized. In practice it was very incomplete and imperfect.

Our pastoral practice is always one of hesitation and groping. We take two steps forward and one step backward. What we do is not brilliant, and not triumphalistic. It is not intended to be a blueprint for anyone else. It is only an experience lived by many sisters and brothers, but it is lived in their very flesh. As I examine it, with my own eyes and from my own outlook, I find that I can offer it as an example of one journey among so many others, and thereby try to be a help to others as others are a help to us.

15

A QUANTUM LEAP

Our ten-year effort had made a contribution to our oneness, in the form of a kind of joint pastoral ministry. But this oneness had not arisen out of an absorption, or organized conquest, of the grass roots. It had arisen out of a reflection on the pastoral practice of the grass roots. And especially it had arisen out of a reflection by the parish and diocesan staffs.

Little by little, in our work, we were discovering that the base community is more than just the base community. It is the base *church* community. This was not discovered by everyone at once. Some never agreed with this at all. And there were still many gray areas, question marks, and mysteries.

But as I see it, we discovered that the base church communities are those geographical spaces, whether on the outskirts of cities or in the bush, where persons strike up a relationship of solidarity, under many different forms, without being explicitly aware of it. They visit with one another, they help one another, they know who has been born, who has died, who has gotten married, who has gone south, who is back, and so on. These are all signs of solidarity in community, and they mean that CEBs are being formed, even if no one has a developed psycho-social awareness of the fact.

Within these communities, gathered around the word and summoned by the word, little living churches are born at the grass roots.

In the light of the word of God, these groups read, discuss, debate, and analyze life. In reading life, they discover the *misery* that gnaws the flesh of their brothers and sisters. The word of God puts the love of God in their hearts. God is their Father, and simply cannot accept a misery that gnaws the flesh of God's daughters and sons.

At this point we became aware of a certain obstacle. Perhaps it was because of the way evangelization had been done in the past. In any case, we realized, we had been persuaded that the cause of our misery was "natural," cosmological. And only God could change what came from nature—*we* could not.

We had to make a quantum leap. The community, reading its situation in the light of the word, had to discover, little by little, that the cause of its misery was *human,* was sociological. If men and women had created misery, men and women united in community, having the living God in their midst as their strength, could remove the causes of that misery. Conclusion: we must undertake a struggle against misery on the community level.

But we went further in our community practice.

We discovered that, if we read the reality of our situation with a twin regard, a double view—that of faith enlightened by the word of God, and that of social analysis, joining science to experience— we learned that misery is not simply caused by humans, it is caused by humans *organized in an oppressive class.* Now, if what we had to face was oppression organized by a class, then we had to organize the struggle of the oppressed.

Organization beyond community boundaries meant a union. Those who practiced the trade of farm workers would unite in a trade union.

The base community wages no struggle in behalf of the union movement. It neither promotes nor directs such a struggle. This is not its task. But it does stimulate the awareness of union militants, so that they, moved by their faith, which operates at the heart of their class commitment, may wage, with their comrades, a struggle against all oppression in loyalty to the gospel and to the people of the countryside.

The "class struggle" of which I speak has no reference to philosophical or scientific theories of class struggle. I am referring to a simple fact of daily experience: there are mechanisms of exploitation at work, wielded by persons who benefit from them as members of a dominant class.

The struggle is initiated and maintained by those who are organized in an oppressive class.

We went further, in the process of the small, vital base churches. The Christian laborers of the basic church communities, in their struggle against organized oppression, discovered, through their struggle for unionism, that out beyond the union struggles there are political centers of decision-making that are more powerful than the unions. The 1980 strike by the ABC metal workers showed this very clearly. The threat to frame the president of CONTAG—the National Confederation of Farm Workers—reinforced this expression.

The metal workers' proposal was a just one, and strictly legal. And yet their leaders ended up in jail and the strike collapsed. Certain centers of political decision-making and military power are out of reach of union strength.

Facing the facts, the communities gradually initiated a base-level political practice and a partisan political option. This base-level political practice is like the alphabet. It has to be learned in a kind of "grade school." Before you do anything else, you have to learn political maturity, where you acquire a critical political conscience. Some day the communities will be able to share in the overall political process, as true agents of this process, as its active protagonists. This is our hope, our solid hope.

16

BASE COMMUNITIES AND POLITICAL PRACTICE

Is the diocese simply turning the CEBs into schools of political practice?

Let me cite some extracts from an interview published in the Brazilian press on April 15, 1969.

> *Interviewer:* Is there a difference in the commitments of bishops, priests, and laity to the liberation struggle?
>
> *Bishop Fragoso:* It seems to me that the struggle for liberation is an objective held in common by priests, lay persons, and bishops. We accept the demand of the workers and *camponeses* that they be allowed to live in a free, just world of sisters and brothers. We accept this demand in solidarity with them.

We are all comrades in these struggles. All our efforts converge on the same objective, and our respective priority tasks are complementary.

The workers and *camponeses* are directly involved in the worker movement and the rural movement. They respond to the exigencies of their human dignity and their work by responsible options that, in their adult consciences, will lead to liberation.

Everything antihuman, antipeople, antiworker, or antirural they have to reject. They have to see clearly and move with courage.

They cannot afford to lose sight of their unity in the struggle. Without this unity the struggle will not be effective.

As citizens of the world, and brothers and sisters of other men and women—even of those who unjustly exploit them—they have no right to harbor hatred in their heart. But it would be a betrayal of everything in their awareness of one another as sisters and brothers to yield to an accommodation with injustice, or not resist the yoke imposed on them by inhumane systems or structures.

As Christians, they take up the liberation struggle in the same way as others do, and along with others, in the name of their commitment to Christ. They are motivated by the word of the Lord.

The priest's job, as I see it, is to educate the worker in the faith. His task is to raise the consciousness of both industrial workers and farm workers by sending them back to the source of their Christian vitality in the sacraments, especially the Eucharist, and by making a prophetic denunciation of whatever oppresses and marginalizes them—then too by his explicitly dissociating himself from all forms of imperialism and discrimination.

If it were to be indispensable, in some circumstances or other, that a priest engage in concrete forms of struggle for liberation, naturally he should do so, but only in communion—brotherly fellowship and contact—with his presbyterate, his fellow priests, with his bishop at their head.

And the bishop? It seems to me that a bishop's tasks are the same as a priest's, with one extra: the exercise of his charism of unifying the presbyterate and the diocesan church.

Interviewer: What is the difference between a prophetic commitment and an ideological commitment?
Bishop Fragoso: In all the events, today, and in all the people, you can find the Lord—who is given, is revealed, in certain signs that challenge us and educate us, and bring it about that everything—even sin—will converge for the increase of the kingdom of God.

To the prophet falls the task of shedding light on the deeper meaning of human activity—shedding light on the Lord's continuous, ongoing Easter. The prophet grasps the calls that are hidden, and manifested, in the signs of the times. Prophets educate their brothers and sisters to a sensitivity to what the Lord is constantly telling us.

The prophet's basic reference is to God's overall project for everything, in the light of faith.

Per se, that rules out any sectarianism.

An ideological option is tied to such and such societal structures, and its objective is to transform the existing ones. It always includes a concrete, relative, "revisable" program. It can easily go sectarian. It tends to exclude other ideologies.

Both the bishop and the priest, in the exercise of their prophetic mission, ought to examine all ideological options in the light of faith, respect them, and help their advocates to come to grips with the universal objective of the liberation of all human beings in Christ.

Many of us, including myself, have come to the firm conclusion that *faith without political practice is dead.*

In the diocese of Crateús, those in the community groups who have a clear view of the social challenge of all the things that crush their sisters and brothers express their faith, make it visible, in deeds—political practice.

To me, it's clear that the only place that faith can be actualized is in the human community, the political community. Christians have to "real-ize" their faith, actualize it—and the only place they can do that is in *the world of the political.*

Political practice in the base communities is not primarily a matter of partisan politics. It is primarily a matter of the organized quest for the common good. This is a call, a right, a grave duty imposed by the gospel. And it is incumbent on all Christians. This is the only sense in which it is true to say that the political struggle, or political practice, is being organized by our communities. Really, all we do in our communities in the way of politics is give persons the ABCs—their grade-school education in politics. They have to extend that on their own, in other expressions, movements not directly tied to the base communities. In the base communities militant Christians see their hope nurtured. They have their vision cleared up, their faith vision. They practice reading the reality of their whole situation in the light of the word of God. They celebrate their passion and their liberation, with the whole church.

And here we have the most profound, most demanding, challenge of all: the continuous dovetailing of faith and political practice.

Christians have to live their faith in a political community. There is no other place to live it. Some want to take Christians out of the political community so they can be "holy." This is sheer idiocy. This is idealism. It has nothing to do with God's plan.

The deep source of motivation for political practice, as far as God's plan is concerned, is faith. Faith motivates Christians— "moves" them, then—to make a commitment to political practice, in loyalty to the gospel and the people. This is what they must do, as citizens of the human community, in order to become co-responsible with their brothers and sisters. Even if they did not have faith, they would be under an obligation to make this commitment. How many there are in the world who say they have no faith and yet who dedicate themselves to political practice to the death!

Meanwhile, the deepest motivation in us is sprung from God's free revelation, as we read it with the eyes of faith.

But faith not only moves Christians, it gives them a *gospel* motivation. Faith points to a "horizon," shows them a horizon, which we call *God's definitive project.* God is beyond history. This horizon is a permanent call, then. It mobilizes Christians to commit themselves to each one's own partisan political practice. This horizon must be incarnated in base-level political projects, national and international.

At the same time, every political incarnation of God's project limits and impoverishes that project. And so the faith horizon becomes a critical light, a critical force, to help us perceive that these *attempts,* necessary though they may be, are all provisional. They are always replaceable by new attempts, new projects.

And so, in faith, we interconnect this horizon, this utopian proposal, with political practice. The horizon is God's dream, being actualized in history little by little. Only beyond history will it be actualized definitively.

Then thirdly—besides moving Christians, and showing them the horizon to move toward—faith accompanies the process of political practice by encouraging a *conversion of heart.*

Christians who are loyal to their faith will never be moved by hatred, revenge, ambition, exploitation, the desire for unjust profits, or the wish to climb over others to get to the top. What moves Christians is their commitment to their brothers and sisters. Christians are called to a comradely sharing of all that they have. Whatever they have been given has been given them both for themselves and for others, and should be shared.

Faith purifies our heart, giving us the capacity to accept others, however different they may be from ourselves, in profound respect for their identity as persons, in respect for their autonomy in making options. For Christians, then, who are moved by their faith, it will appear normal, in political practice, that their comrades, whom they love sincerely and without limit, will make partisan political options different from their own.

In my view, this interconnection between faith and political practice must be subjected to continual revision. It touches upon a mystery, something beyond our ken. This "dovetailing" needs God's light, as well as our own humble, ongoing attempt at synthesization.

But I am working at all this in a very modest way. What I am saying here has already been said, by brilliant theologians, much better than I have said it. I am only trying to apply what they have shared with us, on the level of our diocesan pastoral practice.

I think that the *political space* for an apprenticeship in democratic political practice—or political community practice, or political practice of fellowship—ought to be furnished by political communities, by popular movements, by society, and not specifically and primarily by the church. But the Brazilian political regime marginalized the popular masses for sixteen years. It was frightened out of its wits by any enlightenment or organization among the *camponeses*. There was scarcely any hope that a strangled national political community would offer the space for this exercise that the masses have a right to.

We could scarcely hope for anything from Brazilian *economic* forces—whether completely unrestrained and laissez-faire, "modernizing," or neocapitalistic. All of them were "concentrationist" by their very nature, and deliberately so, doling out to the masses only the superfluities—the crumbs that fall from the tables of the great. They never think the pie has become big enough to share with others.

Our *political* parties, right or left, have been controlled by authoritarian power and have often been dictatorial, or "populist," in their method. Populism tries to lead the people the way populists think the people should go. Populism has never had the patience to listen to the people, to let the people develop its own leadership out of its own practice, never had the patience to stick close to popular practice and be committed to the people. And so populism imposes leaders vertically—especially "intellectuals"— who draw up beautiful base-level documents, lovely projects for the people, but who never have the patience to rouse themselves, *with* the people, to the experience of co-responsibility.

No one was furnishing any base-level space. And the church— not *all* priests and bishops, of course—is convinced that the people has a right to it. So the church has offered the people a base-level political space. But the church may not allow itself to forget that it has no right to maneuver the political process.

17

IN QUEST OF CO-RESPONSIBILITY

From 1964 onward we have been concerned with co-responsibility in the diocese.

By a very special grace of God I was able to take part in the Second Vatican Council, held from 1962 to 1965.

We came to a deeper vision of the church during those four years, especially in the document entitled *Lumen Gentium*—"Light of Peoples." The governing function of the church, understood as evangelical service to the whole community, service in the spirit of the gospel to those who believe in Jesus Christ, is entrusted to the whole episcopate, in co-responsibility. It is to the episcopate as a body, as the successor of the "apostolic college," the apostles as a body, that the whole community of those who believe in Jesus Christ is entrusted. At their head is the pope, with the grace of headship, of being the "principle" of unity, with the charism of "confirming his sisters and brothers in the faith" as successor of Peter.

Between the pope and the episcopate a "collegiality" obtains—a co-responsibility. The church is not governed by the pope alone. Of course, neither is it governed by the rest of the episcopate without the pope.

We do not have very many mechanisms in the church for exercising this collegiality, very many ways of rendering it visible. The special Synod of Bishops that took up the matter of collegiality was not able to make any substantial concrete proposals.

49

I think it is urgent that the "particular churches"—the dioceses—begin the direct exercise of co-responsibility, base-level collegiality, on their own initiative. We are trying to do this in Crateús.

My first concern was to bring the priests into pastoral planning and pastoral decision-making. Early in 1965, when I had my first meeting with the clergy, I invited a planning expert to join us. He showed us his methodology and helped set up some trial parish planning. This was the first time any parish planning had been attempted. There had never been any overall pastoral strategy. All priests worked by themselves, and without consulting the laity of their parishes. This was the first step for them, and I think it should be evaluated as a transitional step.

Beginning with the second and third years, lay persons began to come to our diocesan meetings. At first we invited persons, especially women and girls, who had no jobs outside the home, or who could take time off to spend a whole week with us. They would attend the diocesan assembly and we would plan things together.

Later, gradually, we managed to have much broader representation. Recently our assemblies have been made up mostly of grassroots militants, with the clergy in the minority. Because we wanted to help the laity acquire a critical awareness, we could not have the priests running the meetings, in the old clerical way. They were full participants, and as co-responsible as anyone else, but they could no longer "clericalize" the proceedings of the assemblies.

Little by little the priests of the diocese, and later the nuns and more active lay persons, took part in all discussions bearing on general decisions, or the creation of new pastoral projects, or the assignment of priests and pastoral teams.

And so the bishop and his chancery were dropping their authoritarian reins, and diocesan co-responsibility was taking over. When the bishop had made decisions alone, grave problems could be "solved" in a matter of minutes. After the priests, nuns, and laity were brought into the discussions, things slowed down, sometimes a great deal. For example, we discussed the reassignment of pastoral ministers in light of the needs of various areas of the diocese. We did this for six years, and came up with *one* project—on a trial basis!

All of this is an exercise in patience—something to which we impatient ones are not accustomed.

Co-responsibility leads to the modification and moderation of an authoritarian style in the diocese. The bishop is no longer the chief, simply using his canonical powers to make decisions. He could be. He still has the canonical right to be. But it seemed to me that from a pastoral viewpoint the service to be rendered by authority in the spirit of the gospel meant that the bishop would have to walk with priests, nuns, and laity in co-responsibility. So I ought never to intervene as bishop—only as fellow wayfarer. Of course I still had freedom of conscience to intervene, in the name of the gospel, were it to be necessary. But when the eyes of all of the priests, nuns, and lay persons couldn't see clearly, would the bishop's eyes get any better vision of things? The bishop receives no special inspiration of the Holy Spirit where *certitude* is concerned, when a whole diocese is uncertain. And so the direct interference of the bishop is scarcely ever necessary.

This experiment has not always been as calm and peaceful as I may make it sound. It cost me a profound interior "dismantling." I received my seminary training under a very saintly rector, a true man of God, Monsignor José Tibúrcio de Miranda. He was a priest of deep faith, a contemplative, who spent some three hours a day before the Blessed Sacrament. When he grew old, he entered the Blessed Sacrament Fathers, a white-haired, altogether humble novice in a group of minors. He never gave a talk without preparing it. He lived in poverty. He was a fine, great person, and greatly respected.

But he did not share authority, and he engaged in little dialogue with his subordinates. When I was a deacon, some of my fellow seminarians and I would be sitting in the recreation room talking, and Monsignor Tibúrcio walked by, his umbrella on his arm and his wide-brimmed, black clerical hat in his hand. We all stopped talking and rose from our places. When he was no longer in view, we sat down again and resumed our conversation.

Monsignor Tibúrcio gave me an authoritarian vision of the church, and a view of authority that demanded rigid discipline. Authority was watchful, and strong, and would brook no deviations in the name of personal liberty.

This was how I was trained. And so I had a concept of priestly and episcopal authority that firmly maintained unity throughout a diocese. Then I gradually came to see that co-responsibility required a *sharing* of the service of authority with the presbyterate, the nuns, the laity, the communities. And I was left without a pretext for considering myself "the authority" in the diocese.

But in the course of this journey with my brothers and sisters, I felt as if something were being destroyed inside me—a scheme of things that had been so lovingly constructed by such holy men, my former superiors. I felt as if a kind of anarchy had been sown in the diocese. I no longer had any control.

18

UNITY AS CHALLENGE

The experience of living the charism of unity is a most difficult challenge. This is a charism that I have never been able to put into practice as well as I should like.

There is a style of authority—an external style, imposed vertically from without—that enables a person to project perfect, spellbinding images of things. This style of authority can impose unity from without. But evangelical unity—pastoral unity, ecclesial oneness—must spring from an interior discovery, from a profound conviction of the heart.

I am speaking of a real discovery, something revealed by faith. Jesus Christ joins us together in such a way that we become *one.* This oneness is per se indestructible: it is a radical oneness, an ontological oneness. *We are one in Christ!*

We are called on to accept the visible consequences of this unity. We discover that Jesus has already actualized this oneness in us, and that we are under the obligation to render it visible in the community experience of the church.

My effort to be the "principle of unity" of my particular church has consisted in an attempt to create a space for open discussion of diocesan pastoral problems by all—and not to come to a decision without discussion, and a certain basic convergence of views.

The bishop is not the head of a faction, a sect, or a party. He should be what God intended him to be: the *servant of the people,* the servant of a diocesan church. All have the right to be accepted in this church just as they are. The "progressives," the "moderates," the "conservatives"—all should be accepted and welcomed by the bishop, and he should try to understand them, discover the truth in them, and determine to what extent that truth can be harmonized with everyone else's truth for the good of the whole diocesan church in its service to the people. Even the "conservatives," and even the most "traditionalist" of them, have charisms from the Spirit that are useful for the good of the whole. It is the bishop's task to be open of heart, to be accepting of all. This is a very demanding task—especially for me, who am a bit radical by temperament, and perhaps a bit sectarian. I am still a long way from the attainment of what God expects of me in the service of diocesan unity.

But diocesan unity is *unity in diversity*—inasmuch as none of the members of the diocesan church, none of the grassroots militants, none of the priests or sisters, and not even the bishop, has the last word, just as none of us has *the* definitive proposal to make, the "absolute project." We all propose trial projects, relative visions of things. It is altogether to be expected that we would welcome someone else's proposal, to see how far it might be able to contribute truth of its own to the project of the future that we are all trying to build.

This effort requires, in me, a constant struggle with the grave temptations of "impressionism." I get a first impression. And I am inclined to form my personal judgment and adopt my attitudes on the basis of that impression. An "impressionistic" judgment can be blinded to truth in others, and this is what sometimes prevents me from accepting those others, accepting them just as they are, and so harmonizing their charisms with everyone else's for the oneness of the whole—and then to "confirm them in the faith" on that basis.

I am inclined to make *snap judgments* about others, and then I have a hard time changing my mind. The way a person appears to me the moment we meet is the way I think of that person from then on. It is a very difficult ascetical exercise for me to try to rid myself of this temptation—a very demanding exercise, and I am not very successful, although I do try, very hard.

God has helped me, and generously, in my struggle with these threats to the exercise of my charism of unity. For example, one of the ways I fight my temptations is to place myself in the presence of the living God. I know God sees me as I am. I cannot create a superficial "me" to relate to God with. I'm still the deep, hidden "me," with all its attitude of defensiveness. I stand naked before God, asking for enlightenment, that I may understand the truth that there is in others. I try to review everything I have seen that is good in the persons I too easily think of as "adversaries," those I have antipathy for, those I'm "allergic to."

This effort of mine, and God's grace, help me considerably to see my own truth and the truth of others. And I am also helped to accept the truth of others, so as to be able to harmonize it with the whole truth of my particular church, as its principle of unity.

I say all this in rather orderly fashion. But in practice it is very flawed, imperfect, and groping. As I say, the challenge of the unity of the particular church, at the hands of the bishop's charism and mission, is no easy one. A reconciliation of the exercise of authority with the acceptance of others, in their differences, exceeds our joint power of decision taken in itself. It is lost in the mystery of the living God, the incarnate God. God incarnate in humanity may have a proposal that is crystal-clear in itself, but above our capacity for understanding. The exercise of authority, and the living of the charism of oneness, are bound up with both the human and the divine. This is a human-and-divine mission, and hence somewhat lost in mystery.

Jesus' authority was mighty. At the same time it was tender and accepting. Jesus is the one who will not break the bruised reed or extinguish the smoking flax. But he is also the demanding one, and he acts as Yahweh acted with Moses—asking unreserved faith, amidst a cloud of ignorance.

Moses received the order from God to strike the rock, once, so that water would gush forth. Moses wasn't too sure it would work. He struck once. Then he struck again. He had challenged God's absoluteness, you might say. And so after forty years of marching through the desert, with all the pain and anguish of it, and getting as far as the mountain of Moab where he could see the promised land from afar, Moses heard these terrible words from God: "There is the promised land. But you shall not enter it. You doubted my word."

God is demanding, then. God's authority is total, for each and every person. At the same time God is immensely tender and accepting.

The synthesis of both of these two traits—demand and tenderness—is realized in the human-and-divine Jesus. The synthesis is historical actuality. But for a poor sinner its realization is hard and demanding. And it has to be begun again and again as we zigzag along.

19

MOVING FROM THE MIDDLE TO THE MARGIN

During the pastoral pilgrimage of the diocese of Crateús, the central diocesan agencies, which had been conceived in response to the needs of the people but without the concrete, organized participation of the people, were gradually decreasing in number and importance.

The church of Crateús, with all its limitations and sins, had no intention of being fascist, organizing everything by top-to-bottom imperation. It wanted to be a leaven, promoting consciousness of the liberation established in history by Jesus Christ. It was trying to be an *efficacious sign* of the radical, revolutionary transformation of history.

It was, and is, trying to be a church with the face of a suffering people organizing for liberation. We have arrived at this option by "moving from the middle to the margin." I can't claim that this is the option of the whole diocese, or even of all the higher authorities of the diocese. Some accept it, others do not. But it seems to me that we are heading toward a basic convergence.

We are trying, at least as I see it, to come to the following decision. We may start out with a love for the people, and create central service agencies, but if we do so without the participation of the people at every stage, then, in the light of what we know now, we have not done as we should. We have no right to create "vertical agencies." God asks us to have the historical patience to walk hand in hand with the people, to the end that, from out of the people, and from the practice of the people, new coordinations and interconnections may arise, on the intercommunitarian, regional, and parochial levels of diocesan pastoral activity.

This emergence of the pastoral ministry from the base level, from the grass roots, is a long process. How long, we do not know. We are still searching. Our diocesan pastoral agencies have been reduced to three: the Diocesan Pastoral Council, the Diocesan Administrative Council, and the Provisional Committee for Rural Pastoral Ministry.

The Pastoral Council is made up of priests and parish and diocesan pastoral leaders. Each parish chooses its council member, and trains him or her in a process that is now under serious review.

The Administrative Council sees to the general management of the diocese.

We are looking for a way to interrelate these two councils. We have not found one. Each of the two should serve the other in some way. The administration of the diocese should be pastoral, and so the Administrative Council should be at the service of the Pastoral Council. But the pastoral ministry requires management, and depends on it. So these two councils should serve and benefit each other.

Our critical reflection on the Diocesan Pastoral Council has led us to pose some serious questions. Some of the priests and laity of the diocese were saying, "The Pastoral Council is a monstrosity. All the other central service organizations have been abolished, and their functions have been absorbed by this one council. No wonder it is full of conflicts and cross-purposes!"

This group has persuaded us to undertake a radical critical review of the Diocesan Pastoral Council.

On the administrative side, we are working in the direction of co-responsibility. First, the diocesan "center" has tried to be honest with the parishes. For example, it worked out a diocesan budgetary plan and proposed it to the ten parishes. We were ready to accept well-founded criticism and make any necessary modifications. But because this was the first time we were trying this, the parishes were not accustomed to making critical examinations of a proposal. They made a few minor observations, but without much content. And the diocesan budgetary project was approved "as is."

The next year we presented our accounts to the parishes, asked for criticism, and presented a new diocesan budget proposal. This time there was a little more participation.

With the first steps taken, then, we now invited the ten parishes to make their own individual budget proposals for the year, submit them to one another for criticism, and thus begin to take part in the actual process of budgetary planning. By year's end, all this was done.

Today we have settled down to a routine here. The diocesan "center" and the ten parishes meet once a year to submit their accounts, their respective budgetary proposals, and their theological reflection on the participatory administrative process.

The Provisional Committee for Rural Pastoral Ministry, established in 1978, is presently looking for the best way to encourage and improve pastoral ministry as conducted by grassroots communities—and working toward the day when the militant grass roots can undertake their own coordination, and, together with the diocesan officials in charge of pastoral ministry, form their own, permanent, Committee for Rural Pastoral Ministry.

20

IN QUEST OF A "REFORMULATION AT THE ROOTS"

Looking at all our challenges en bloc, the real question surfaces: "Church of Crateús, what is your self-image? What is your self-awareness? In all your structures, in all your various sectors, are you being a service to the people in the spirit of the gospel? Are you being a servant? Are you being poor?"

We find that we must have a common or convergent awareness of being church in order to make the modifications that we need in the ecclesial service structures.

In order to answer our "real question," we are moving along two paths—seemingly parallel, but tending eventually to converge.

The first path is that of the *base-level church communities,* the CEBs. It seems to me that the diocesan church is in the process of a long gestation. I do not know when the birth will be. But what is going on is the forming of a new face of the church. I call it a *popular church.* That is, this will be a church born in the life of the people, by the power of the Spirit that leads this people in the faith.

The popular church will be a revolutionary one—at the heart of the traditional church. It will be the occasion of profound changes, including structural ones—not changes in the basic structure that Jesus Christ left to us and willed as definitive, but changes in cultural, historical structures that the church itself has created down through the ages.

Representatives of the CEBs made the selection of those who would see to the necessary steps in the direction of a *Diocesan Assembly of Base Communities*. It is these persons' task to coordinate all the preparations for such an assembly, run the assembly itself, and then write up conclusions. It is an autonomous process, as it seems to us that it ought to be.

The diocesan church, through its principal leaders, will keep abreast of the process, but without "directive intervention." They will want to be present to the process as fellow wayfarers along this pedagogical path to service.

The second path is that of the great *traditional church* of Crateús. To this church belong not only the little grassroots church cells, but all the other sectors of our pastoral work, from the most progressive to the most moderate. They include parochial and diocesan structures, the chancery, the popular masses in their religious practice, and so on.

We intend to try to answer that basic question of ours. We shall try and try again. I asked a group of persons to speak out freely as to what they thought of the diocesan church. Their responses have been made into a leaflet, and sent out to the parishes with the request that they be studied and commented on in writing. Next we shall put all these critical reflections in some synthetic order and return them to the parishes.

As a second step, we are trying to identify what we call, ambiguously enough, I suppose, "pastoral zones." These are interparish pastoral work groups, from works-of-mercy associations to the Rural Pastoral Committee. A special group has been set up for these pastoral zones. It will call each zone together at the proper moment to ask this question: "Is your sector struggling for a church of the poor in its apostolic practice? Is it committed to the people's liberation?"

After the separate meetings, there will be a general meeting of all zones, to get an overview of their apostolic practice and their possible integration into the overall pastoral effort.

Next, continuing the process—in ways that we have not yet discerned or chosen—will we eventually get to a "general synod," or general "diocesan assembly," with the base communities and all the other service sectors and structures participating? Will we arrive at a basic convergence on the image we have of ourselves as church? Will we come to a reorientation of the whole diocese toward the "popular face of the church"?

At the heart of such discoveries, and in light of them, we shall have the right to carry out the necessary structural reforms. Will the *diocesan curia* continue as it is, or will it be different? Will the Diocesan Administrative Council continue as it is? What changes will we be making in the Diocesan Pastoral Council? Or should it disappear?

We are in this stage of quest, of search. We do not know very well where we will end. We are in the twilight of faith.

We seek a kind of revision, but we do not yet have clear evidence of just how to effectuate it. We have as yet no developed, clear project before us against which to measure our progress. We only have a kind of general proposition to work with. It may be that, along these pathways, we may succeed in developing a more organic, more realistic church project—a project with the participation of the whole diocese. It may be. But we may also be working along pathways that we shall have to follow for many years to come. We have many uncertainties, many insecurities, about the future.

I am not making comparisons with any other diocese. Surely there must be pastoral processes far more meaningful for today's church than ours. I am only making my contribution to the search.

PART TWO

AN ATTEMPT AT
INTERPRETATION:
REFLECTIONS ON BUILDING
A CHURCH OF THE POOR

The story I've been telling you took a great deal longer to happen than it did to tell. You can't get a sixteen-year history into a two-hour conversation, or into the pages of a little book, and include all the peaks and valleys, all great hopes and great sufferings.

This same story could be told by the priests of the diocese—by the older priests who were in the thick of things at the beginning and who are retired now, or by priests long in the ministry, or newly-ordained priests—or by the laity of the communities, or by the practicing masses of the people, or by the middle-class elite—and you'd get a basically different story every time.

I'm speaking for myself, then. I have no authorization to represent the thinking, the discoveries, of my companions in the struggle.

In the course of my narrative, I introduced certain value judgments on our pastoral work, to justify the positions we took.

Now, in this second part of my book, I am going to undertake an attempt at interpretation.

1

PROJECT: A POPULAR CHURCH

This story, it seems to me, contains a hidden project or "model" of church. By "model" I only mean a project that actually takes flesh in practice. I do not mean an example for others to follow. The word "model" is ambiguous, and so I want to specify very clearly what I mean by it. I mean the kind of model that emerges from within a practice, such that we reflect on it, collectively, in an ongoing fashion.

It seems to me that what we had in Crateús—and still have, by and large—is a traditional church. To my way of thinking, the church of Crateús is, in the main, traditional, conservative, and moderate. It is not very revolutionary. It is not an advanced church.

The church of Crateús combines two *historical images of church:* that of a *pyramid,* and that of a *center-with-periphery.*

In the former, the universal church is thought of as a kind of pyramid. At the top you have the hierarchy, with the mission to teach, and the assistance of the Holy Spirit to guarantee its authentic, infallible interpretation of the deposit of faith in the areas of beliefs and morals. At the bottom are the people, the faithful, who must accept, in faith and unfailing obedience, whatever the hierarchy proposes as "of faith," *de fide.* The faithful will "sanctify themselves," achieve holiness, through the exercise of this obedient acceptance of what the hierarchy proposes to them.

In the second image, that of "center-with-periphery," the universal church is divided into a center, which makes the decisions and watches over the fidelity of the other churches, the peripheral churches. The local church is a microcosm or copy of the universal church. Local churches are like satellites, revolving about the center. Local churches, the base churches, have no autonomy other than that granted or conceded by the central church. In this sense, then, they are not fully church.

Crateús, like many other places in Brazil and throughout the world, still has a *clerical model of church.* The clergy is the center. It holds the supreme power of decision-making. It calls on the faithful for help. The laity collaborates with the clergy and its mission, the mission of the institution.

This model revolved around the persons of the bishop and the pastor. The pastor was in charge of the "mother church," with its outlying churches and chapels. He reared the laity in the faith. He taught through his preaching religious education, the sacraments, and parish groups, with the final decision always reserved to himself. He visited the outlying chapels at regular intervals, and called the faithful together regularly to receive the sacraments and hear the word, without any active participation on their part. The priest was the church and so the people were convinced that when there was no priest, the whole church collapsed and died.

We still have this traditional model in Crateús. The greater proportion of the popular masses still demand the continuous presence of a priest. If Father isn't there, discouragement sets in. Still, little by little, in the nuclei consisting of the more conscious base communities, with their more mature practice, lay persons are beginning to discover that *they* are the church, that they are co-responsible, and can take up the responsibility of being-church without depending completely on a priest. They still feel the need of a priest and his priestly mission. In fact, they feel it more than ever. But they no longer accept a domineering clergy, one that gathers all ministries into its own hands.

It seems to me, as I consider this history of ours over the last sixteen years, that the model of church that we are attempting to incarnate, however imperfectly, the model that we seek to have merge from within the great traditional church, is the new image—and at the same time the old biblical image—proposed to us by the Second Vatican Council. The church is a *people co-responsible for its history as church.* At the heart of the church, God raises up *ministers* for the evangelical service of the whole people.

This new image applies to the universal church, to each local church, and to each little, living CEB.

I view the base church community as a genuine church. As such, it must be a people co-responsible for its history, having ministries within it constituting the evangelical service of the whole. We can no longer have simply the "leaders" and the "led," at contrary poles of an authoritarian system.

Humbly and sadly, I must confess that, here again, we constantly fall back into our old tradition of central authority and peripheral obedience. It is a tradition of very long standing, and not only the bishop and priests, but the lay animators—the leaders, the community directors—are continuously tempted to live the model that is still stuck in their secular memory.

The new model of church that we are trying to live in Crateús will not become a *stable model* for at least four or five decades. It seems to me that a principle of mass psychology is valid here: the masses have acquired a long *memory*—the memory of their grandparents, great-grandparents, and so on—and of the experience that these have seen or that others in turn have passed on to them. When the masses act, discuss, converse, and reflect, these processes are always rooted in traditional models in their memory. Now, the only model of church they have ever seen and practiced, their whole life long, is the *clerical* model. The model of a co-responsible people is still in its first beginnings, a scant ten years old. It has not taken root in the memory of the masses.

We shall have need of greater patience. We are going to fall back hundreds of times. May God give us the grace of an ongoing critical watchfulness—seeing that it is God who asks of us this service, this vehement asceticism.

2

FROM THE VANTAGE
OF THE POOR

This model of people-church, then, is still in its gestation in Crateús.

The whole church is called to become the *people of God,* a people called by the word and testifying to Jesus Christ, its Lord, in whom it believes.

For me, the *popular church* is the church of the oppressed, the little ones, the poor, the weak, coming together in their grassroots groups that we call *base church communities.* And so, at the heart of the great people-church, the *popular church* is emerging.

I have the impression that we in the diocesan church of Crateús are living something of the tension experienced by the universal church today.

At Vatican II, I witnessed two popes, some twenty-five hundred bishops, and more than seven hundred experts in the theological sciences, coming to some basic conclusions. Here is one of the conclusions at which we arrived: *the church is a co-responsible people.* The government of the church is shared, in collegiality, by the one who holds the "primacy"—the mission of confirming and strengthening his brothers and sisters in the faith, the mission of being the center or principle of unity—and his brother bishops the world over. Every local church is the universal church in a given locus. It is not the periphery of a center, but rather expresses and incarnates the universal church, in communion with all its fellow churches.

All this was revealed and declared, with the special assistance of the Holy Spirit, by the pope and the episcopate gathered in ecumenical council.

Meanwhile, after the council, we are witnessing some attempts to rehabilitate the traditional models of church.

We have not yet discovered the mechanisms for actualizing, in the church, the Vatican II declarations on the nature of church— which are also old declarations, rediscovered in this new *prise de conscience* of ours. We have been so accustomed to the pyramidal, or else center-and-periphery, model of church, that it is very difficult to actualize the Vatican II old-and-new image of church in new structural concrete expressions, new functional mechanisms.

All of us, bishops and everyone else, have become used to being peripheral churches that run to the central church in Rome for everything. We ran there for *complete instructions.* During my seven years as vice-rector of the seminary in Paraíba, I remember that we would receive ready-made detailed sets of instructions, all the way to such matters as the number of Latin, Greek, and Hebrew classes we were to schedule! The center would pass judgment "objectively." It had a "universal view of things." And so it could send exhaustive instructions to everyone.

But all of this seems to me to run counter to the collegiality, the co-responsibility, the ecclesial fullness, of the local churches. And so we are yielding to the temptation to backslide when we sigh for the good old days. When we go to Rome to visit the pope, we do not feel like brothers visiting a brother. We feel like subjects visiting their ruler, within the workings of a feudal administration and a structurally heavy one at that.

It seems to me that we have not as yet discovered the basic mechanisms that we shall need for the expression of collegiality and co-responsibility in the church. The actual practice of the church contradicts the new practice proposed to us by the spirit of Vatican II. Of course, it is natural for these tensions to exist, even at the level of the local church of Crateús. It is natural for those who are attached to the traditional model, which has made so many saints and been blessed by God for so many centuries, to consider as heretical or schismatic a model of church that is a sincere attempt, even if not perfect, to incarnate the new image proposed by the Vatican Council.

Personally I think that the rediscovery of the church-at-the-base, built on the poor and the lowly, bids fair to shed a flood of light on the church as a whole. It is likely to provoke a structural change, a radical conversion—again, one built on the poor and the little. I think that this is the story of all true collective conversions. Conversion is mediated by the poor and the little, not by the "high and mighty," the top of the ecclesiastical pyramid.

3

THE PROBLEM
OF THE MAGISTERIUM

In the church of Crateús, the magisterium is begininng to be viewed differently, and this is generating tension.

I remember the document of the Second Vatican Council on divine revelation. We had had a certain static view of revelation, and it predominated in the preparatory schema. God's revelation was definitively closed with the death of the last Apostle. The deposit of revelation was thereupon confided for safeguarding and interpretation to the infallible magisterium of the church. The magisterium had the assistance of the Holy Spirit to guarantee its infallibility.

To my way of seeing, we had done little to sound the depths of the meaning of all this. The competency of the infallible magisterium had swollen beyond bounds. Theology was hemmed in, even repressed. There was no openness to theological exploration—attempts at systematic reflection, important as a help to the magisterium. We did not have the courage to accept pluralism, because we were afraid to shake what we imagined to be the fundamental unity of the church.

The hierarchy enjoys the special assistance of God's Spirit to assist its church in matters of faith and morals. But the Spirit is not the monopoly of the hierarchy. The Spirit is communicated, with limitless abundance, to all the particular churches, to all the bases, and especially to humble, simple hearts. The Spirit communicates and gives *intuitions* concerning God's design, God's self-projection—prophetic intuitions on how to read history and events.

The basic mission of the magisterium should be to accept the Holy Spirit, who speaks in all the churches in their diversity. Upon this "prime matter," with its immense variety, the magisterium should exercise its charism of unity, its charism of being the harmonizer of the other charisms bestowed by the Spirit for the good of the church.

The magisterium has not always been good at patience—the patience required for lengthy consultation with local churches. The center was accustomed to send out instructions. There are some fabulous examples. On the occasion of a bishop's visit to the pope and the Holy See—called the visit *Ad Limina Apostolorum,* "to the doorway of the Apostles" Peter and Paul—bishops often cited the experience of their pastoral practice and reflection accumulated over years of loyal devotion, years of experience with sin and with hope. Instead of eagerly and expectantly listening to the bishops, some Roman Congregations simply gave them "orientations," as if the Spirit had already made a special revelation to them.

On the level of the local churches, this generates tension and misunderstanding. And this is the case with the local church of Crateús.

I believe in the irreplaceable charism of the magisterium of the church. I believe in the charism of the infallibility of the church. But I try to understand these charisms as Christ understands them—as Christ, their source, reveals them. And I know that revelation is not grasped once and for all, but through successive *prises de conscience,* or what is called "conscientization," consciousness-raising, throughout history.

The church did not have the same consciousness, the same awareness, of its infallibility when it was just starting out as it did, for example, in 1985. This consciousness is gradual, ongoing.

Theologians—and the small, vital, base churches—can all contribute to the formation of the church's self-awareness.

4

A POPULAR CHURCH?

There are those in Latin America who call this model of church a "popular" church. The word has its ambiguities. And so there are theologians who have written a surprising amount on the "dangers of a popular church"!

To them the popular church looks heretical. Any true church springs from God, is born of God. The popular church springs from the people, is born of the people! It looks like a kind of ideological projection of democracy.

Or else it looks like a schismatic church, because it springs from the people, not the hierarchy. The hierarchy is the visible head of the church, sharing by grace in the headship of Christ.

Or else it looks to them like a politicized church, because it is open to the left, open to a sort of socialist social projection.

Inasmuch as we are dealing with an ambiguous term, then, I have to define what I mean by popular church.

By *popular church* I mean the small base church communities, the CEBs, in the diocese of Crateús and elsewhere, that have not sprung primarily from the orientation and directives of the bishop of the diocese, or from the orientation and directives of pastors, but from the Christian nuclei of natural communities, who have come together to read, meditate, and pray God's word, to let the light of the word shine on the reality of their lives, to celebrate their life and their faith. And from these activities, the light of the word is reflected upon their co-responsibility as church.

Obviously, this work, performed as it is with the assistance of priests and bishops who listen to the people, incorporates the irreplaceable contribution of these priests and bishops as well. But this model is not first and foremost proposed by the clergy, to be applied at the base. It is born of the Spirit of God, who is in the life of the people as in the heart of the pope and the heart of the hierarchy. By the power of the Spirit there emerge, as the *face of the church,* services, the *diakoniai,* the ministries the church needs for its growth precisely as church.

This kind of popular church seems to me to constitute an important alternative in the church of Crateús—an alternative to the traditional model.

I am not trying to hurry things, however. This would be an intervention, all over again, of the hierarchical church in the process taking place in the history of the diocese. It is not my task to implant a new model of church. This would be verticalism again—authoritarian centralism.

I seek only to accompany, to "second," a practice that is being reflected on in the light of faith, along the routes and at the hour determined by the Spirit, in order to discover how the Spirit proposes to reveal the new face of the church that will one day come to light.

I may be wrong. It may even be that this is all just my imagination. I have no hard facts on which to base my anticipation of the future so that I can select the most likely hypothesis. But I find within me a certitude, as strong a certitude as I can have with my imperfections, that this is the model that is being born. We shall see this face some day. Shall *I* see it? I don't know. But the people will see it. For the people continues. I am temporary.

5

HISTORY IN ONE'S HANDS
AND A SURE PATH AHEAD

Some comparisons may be useful in clarifying some aspects of my reflection that might still be vague.

I like to use the comparison of Mary of Nazareth. When she was making her long journey to see her cousin Elizabeth, she was carrying her Son in her womb. Mary of Nazareth was sure that he was going to be born. He was already within her. She could feel him. But what would he be like exactly? How would his face, his eyes, his hair look? She didn't know. But she was sure that, within her, she was carrying her child, and he would be born.

In the same way, we are certain that a popular church is about to emerge. The signs are there. But its actual face has not as yet appeared. I don't know whether the day of its birth is near or far-off. We have to be patient. This is not the moment for an impatient midwife! We have to have patience, and await the hour of the Spirit.

Friends reading this may have the impression that I accept a church born in the life of the people, the poor, the little ones, the *camponeses,* a church sprung up on the outskirts of the great cities—and that I dismiss the divine mission of the hierarchy, the priestly ministry, the theological ministry, and the ministry of religious sisters and brothers—that I dismiss everything except our "communities."

May I say, then, that what seems to be being generated is precisely a new sense of hierarchical, priestly, and religious mission. We are on the verge of rediscovering the gospel meaning of service and ministry. We are about to rediscover the divine meaning of dedication and consecration, especially in the area of celibacy. Celibacy is not the amputation of the physical ability to generate life. Nor is it the rejection of the calling of man and woman to be completed in the married life. Celibacy is first and foremost the acceptance in one's heart, in one's absolute love, of all those who are not loved, with the same tenderness with which their Father loves them. Celibacy is the prioritarian, the preferential acceptance of the unloved, and this with the very tenderness of the heart of the Father.

Inasmuch as the CEBs are made up of the lowly, the unloved, those who find themselves on the margin of historical processes, those who count for nothing, it is they who must have priority in the hearts of the priest, the religious sister or brother, and the bishop. Their consecration to God in celibacy opens their hearts and renders them free to accept the poor with a love like that of the Father for these same persons—with a love in imitation of the Father's love. This is what I mean when I speak of a rediscovery of the meaning of consecration.

More and more, the communities I know are looking for a priest. They need, they want a priest as their brother along their journey. They want a priest to hear them with patience, to discover with them the Spirit present in their life, a priest to be totally consecrated to, especially, the very weakest and most despised members of the community.

The members of base communities are looking more and more earnestly for a priest to celebrate the Eucharist with them. Without a priest they cannot fully celebrate the Eucharist. And they know that they cannot. They have need of a priest to celebrate the sacraments—or if you will, to celebrate the life and liberation of the people through the sacraments. They want a priest to harmonize the sacerdotal ministry with the many ministries taken on by the community.

The popular church is not a threat to the ministry of bishop or priest. It is a grace from the Lord for the rediscovery of the evangelical sense of ecclesial ministries. The CEBs are not squeezing out the hierarchy. They are a mediation for its conversion, its remaking, as servant of the poor.

Insofar as we—bishop, religious, and priests—are willing to cast our lot with the people, for a good long time, and insofar as we are willing to listen to the people, affectionately and lucidly, and insofar as we seek to read in the life of the people the good news that God is communicating to it and to accept that message for our own conversion—in just this far shall we grow in the fullness of grace of our ministry, and actualize our special charism of church.

We must not be afraid. We must be open, and believe in the Spirit, who raises up these small, living churches at the base. The Spirit is more intelligent than we, the bishop, the priests, and the religious!

6

PROJECT FOR SOCIETY

In this story of a diocesan pastoral practice, I think there emerges, little by little, a church model, or a church project. But I think there is a project for a society here, too, underlying all our work.

Obviously, when we talk about the project of a church we are touching on the very nerve of our mission. When we talk about the project of a society, we are not talking about something that it is our mission to develop for the people. This is something the people itself, the human community, must develop, collectively. And Christians have their special task in the process—that of making the connections between faith and political practice, from the motivation, critical horizon, and conversion of heart that is theirs within the development of the project, that the project may be faithful to God's intention, which is a *free people in a free society.*

But what kind of project for society will this be?

The ordinary model of Brazilian society is the capitalistic one. First comes capital, not labor. First comes money, not human beings. First comes profit, not service to the basic needs of the whole people.

In this capitalistic model, there is a very strong tendency for wealth to be concentrated in the hands of a few, an elite. Meanwhile the mechanisms that have been erected—the commercial structures, the relationships of production, exchange, and finance—demand an ever greater concentration. Now, this concentration does not occur innocently, inoffensively. As Pope John

Paul II said in Puebla: "The rich grow richer at the expense of the poor, who grow poorer and poorer."

In Crateús, then, the capitalistic model could not be an alternative, a serious proposal, something to use in our pastoral practice.

I think that there are forces at work for modernization, on the capitalist model, that are applied to intermediate powers like Brazil for their *dependent* modernization.

This modernizing effort fails to resolve the radical contradiction of the concentration of wealth in the hands of elites in society at the cost of the exploitation and marginalization of the majority.

This capitalistic model of society, to my mind, is a blasphemy against God. As it is lived, historically, it is a paradigm that is simply unacceptable to the Christian conscience.

I would go even further. The existing capitalist model is legitimated and justified by the ideologies that are constructed by the dominant classes to make the process acceptable. The capitalist process is soulless and brutal, and feeds on the flesh of the masses. It would not be accepted were it to be proposed crudely and directly. It must be embellished, adorned, made attractive. As a bitter pill is coated and made into a piece of candy, so also are the ideologies of the dominant classes calculated to make the capitalist philosophy acceptable to the popular masses.

It would seem that capitalist ideologies and the capitalist model have little by little entered into the consciousness of the people of the countryside and on the outskirts of the cities of the diocese of Crateús. And they have led this people to be convinced that this is the only way there is. The people must live in the shadow of the great, then, in the shadow of power. Only power has the resources and conditions necessary to liberate the people. This leads the people to try to curry favor among members of powerful families, having them as their patrons and godparents, so that these "relatives" may be their refuge at difficult moments.

Further: practically all the university graduates from the popular masses, who have managed to overcome the obstacles to their rise to success, uproot themselves from the popular milieu and from any involvement with the popular masses. Often they become technocrats who legitimate the established, capitalist order. This is a kind of conscious or unconscious treason of the people.

The capitalist model constitutes no objective hope for the people. The people know that all it can hope for is a palliative. But it needs palliatives in its agonizing situation. And so it runs into capitalism, takes refuge in the shadow of power, makes supplication, becomes subservient, emulative of that power. But to the healthiest, deepest vision in the hearts and awareness of the people, it is clear that the capitalist model is *antipeople.*

From my viewpoint, there is a profound tension between healthy popular aspirations and the capitalist model. This tension bursts into view only at certain moments, when the contradiction of the capitalist system has become so evident that no one can any longer deny it. For example, when the Brazilian economic bubble burst, completely, and the "miracle" evanesced, prices rose giddily while wages stayed very low. Even if you earn ten or twenty times what you were making before, your purchasing power is less now. This contradiction gnaws at the flesh of the people, and foments tension. This tension has not yet flowered into a self-consistent, mature popular struggle, because no solution is in view as far as the people can see. The capitalist system allows the people no space to overcome these tensions.

The church of Crateús is contemplating a model of society in which the people has its voice, just as much a voice as anyone else— not the voice of oppressors and dominators, but simply the voice to which every human person has a basic right.

I am thinking of a *participatory model,* in which popular experience would be considered just as valid, and perhaps more human than technological expertise. The "technological package," as we call it, would be made up not just of elements of scientific technology, produced in the schools, but of the experience of the people as well, as it is gathered and solidified in their own secular milieu.

This popular participation would mean that the people will have to be listened to, in all the projects that concern it—and not out of political strategy or demagoguery, but simply in recognition of the fact that the people is the agent of the political process as much as anyone else. The people must participate, as agent, in all the stages of human development.

7

LISTENING TO THE PEOPLE

How may one seize upon what is soundest in the people's heart in its current condition? What will be the criteria for listening to the people?

I recall an investigation made by SUDENE (Superintendency for Development of the Northeast, a government agency) during a great drought. The SUDENE professional personnel—the "doctors," as the locals call them—came to the Pernambuco area and visited the people of the countryside. "Are you satisfied with what you earn?" they asked. "Yes, doctor," came the answer, "we are satisfied." "Is everything going well, do you think?" "Yes, thank God, everything is going well." And the pollsters return home with the "people's opinion."

Then some bishops and priests came to spend some time with the inhabitants of regions affected by the drought. They said that their wages were not enough to live on, that their wives and children were hungry, that they themselves were highly dissatisfied, that they had no medicine, that they had to work at a great distance from their homes, that all this constituted oppression, and so forth and so on.

Finally, the bishops met with SUDENE, and presented the people's demands. "Your Excellencies are misinformed," came the response. "Our personnel have been to see and listen to the people, and they say just the opposite."

The dwellers of the countryside are much smarter than they are given credit. They have a saying, "An old monkey doesn't stick its hand into a jar." That is, they look, observe, and test the ground for a long time before they say what is really on their minds—before they reveal their true aspirations. They know that sometimes what they're saying is escapism. But they know, too, that if they say what is radically on their minds, they'll be crushed, and that they have no way to resist directly.

One basic criterion, then, for listening to the people correctly will be to listen *with heart and mind—con intelecto d'amore.* The listener must use perspicacity. One who listens acritically or uncritically—naively—will seize on the first impression, and say, "This is what they think." But it is not! This is what they *say,* in order to survive. What they *want,* from the bottom of their hearts, is to *be a people,* to be done *justice,* to be *treated as human beings.*

I have a great deal of confidence in popular wisdom, and very little in the superficial "findings" of polls.

I had an interesting experience at a meeting of CEBs in the very poorest area of the Macambira regions, Serra Grande. About sixty persons had gathered to discuss their situation. They drew up a list of the most crying facts, and they compared them to rotten fruit on a tree. They sketched the tree—the trunk, the soil with the roots, and the branches with the fruit hanging from them.

Then I asked them: "What's the root of this tree, that bears rotten fruit like this?" All replied, "Profit." It was profit in the hands of a few, profit unshared by all who need it, that was at the root of the people's ills.

Another question: "What shall we do with this tree?"

The answer: "Cut it down."

Question: "Why not just prune the branches?"

"No. They'll grow back. You have to pull up the whole thing."

"But it has all those roots!"

"Right. You have to get the taproot—profit."

"Fine. And all these dozens of things you're doing in the communities—are you laying the axe to the root? Or are you spreading manure over the roots?"

They divided up into groups, held their discussions, and returned with an answer: "We're giving the root a chop or two. But mostly we're fertilizing a tree that gives rotten fruit."

"Fine. So the next question is—if you cut this tree down, pull it up by the roots—where are you going to find shade?" Back to the groups.

And the answer came: "We need shade, and we have a right to it. We need a tree. But not this one. Another one."

"Which?"

They sketched a new tree, with fruit they considered good for the life of the people: justice, wages with adequate purchasing power for everyone, land for all who needed land to work, the right to an education, the opportunity to participate in political life, water for everyone, and so on.

And the tree was finished.

"And the root of this new tree?"

"Everybody contributing everything."

It seems to me that they really grasped what it's all about. They had a project, there, down deep inside them, and didn't know how to "put it," how to bring it out. They were embarrassed at not being able to dress things up in pretty language. They'd had no training in literary matters. If they were to put it in some semiliterate way, no one would pay any attention to them. Besides, who wants to look like a dummy? And so they finally put things in a way that would make the great ones pay attention to them—in metaphors and slogans.

It is with perspicacity that one must listen to the people.

8

CHANGING THINGS
AT THE ROOTS

It seems to me that the project that we envisage—or that I envisage, at any rate—calls for a radical change in current society.

There are different kinds of possible changes.

THE BAND-AID PHILOSOPHY

A first type of change is a very common one: we discover a great many instances of injustice and oppression, but fail to perceive the connection among them, and so propose to "remedy" these situations with some form of *aid*. This kind of disconnected, scattered assistance we call "charity" or "charitable works." How often I have seen my brothers and sisters who have a little more money than others having a Christmas party so that they can give clothes or toys to children without any. They make no attempt to learn *why* these children have no clothes at home.

In the joy of our hearts, we seek to receive every sister and brother of ours who is in misery as Christ himself. We don't know how to do it. But we want to do it. We're trying. And we do know one thing. "Aid" isn't the way. We'd be leaving the *system* still manufacturing misery, and we'd be "peacefully coexisting" with it.

REFORMISM

Nor do we want only reforms. We compare present society in our country, or at least in Crateús, with a body, and its many organs. If the body is sound, but an eye hurts, you treat the eye, of course.

But this is why reformism is such a dangerous disease. When you try to treat just certain organs in the social body, leaving the body as a whole to fend for itself, you haven't found the answer. The reformist solution is not the answer. This isn't what we're looking for. We know that, at bottom, the reformist solution doesn't disturb the established "order," doesn't bother the political, economic, and military leadership that foster this "order." No one would ever call us "subversive" if all we did was call for reforms. We wouldn't be going to the heart of the matter. We'd be acting as if the social organism were basically healthy, and only had some sick organs in need of reform. We'd be disturbing no one. We'd be coexisting. We'd be legitimating the established "order" (really, disorder).

RADICAL CHANGE

I find that production, the means of production, commerce and marketing, finance, and the relationships of production, such as we have them, transfer the greater part of the fruit of the honest sweat of human beings to a group not always composed of the ones who do the work. And those who do do the work are deprived of even the bare essentials. For example, when harvest time comes—very hard work—the basic daily wage for farm laborers, even children, is usually not enough to live on for one day. But the whole family has to live on it. And we're told that the problem is being solved!

I am for radical change. In other words, I regard the established "order" as *established disorder,* blasphemy, institutionalized sin. We cannot "peacefully coexist" with that.

And so of course the project for society that I desire is *subversive.* I seek to *subvert the established disorder,* because, radically—at its root—it blasphemes God, and we're committed to God and to this people of God crushed by a capitalist regime.

9

SUBVERSIVE STRUGGLE

I am convinced that it is not the business of the church—the universal church, the diocesan church, or the base church (which we call a base *church* community)—to propose concrete projects for structuring a society. This would be to transform the church into a kind of fascism, for it would be an attempt to organize the whole of society. It would be a new form of theocracy, a new form of clericalism. I don't want the rebirth of clericalism. And so I leave it to the people, trained in the school of its base church communities as well as elsewhere—as long as the training respects the people and makes use of sound pedagogy—to develop, along with experts who have been converted to the people, a project for a participatory society.

I want to be at the service of the people's awareness, of its consciousness. I am not proposing a project for society. I have a vision, in broad outline, of a project for a participatory society. I do not, however, have a concrete model to propose. This is a basic point. My concern is the effectuation of the proper connections between the church project I seek to implant, and the societal project that the people will develop.

Let me clarify my outlook somewhat, to avoid ambiguities.

"Order," for me, denotes a set of social structures in which all persons are treated as *beloved daughters and sons of God,* with full respect accorded their right to *have,* to *know,* and to *act.*

"Disordered" is the concentration of all having, knowing, and acting in the hands of a few, at the expense of the exploitation of all the others.

When what prevails is an established disorder, in which a small group has an easier, privileged political, social, and economic situation by reasoning of mechanisms of exploitation of the people—putting and keeping the people in a situation of misery, which many call "order," the "free world," or "Western Christian civilization"—a committed faith will move us to a struggle in solidarity with the people, a struggle that will be radically transforming.

10

NONVIOLENT STRUGGLE

When I speak of destruction, tearing down, and radical change, I am not referring to an armed struggle on the part of the people.

I am referring to the opportunity of persons in the base communities and popular movements to acquire a critical awareness, to organize, and to demand respect for their dignity.

My option is for *nonviolence*. I believe that the most radical struggle for justice ought to be waged in respect for every human being, and for the truth that there is in each, whoever he or she may be. For this reason, I cannot accept any process involving arms, institutionalized violence, or violent repression.

In our practical experience with the popular masses in our region, we of the official church have not trained them to be militant. And yet we call the pilgrim church the *church militant*. So we do intend to train them for a battle. But it will be the battle for the kingdom of God, for the incarnation of justice in every human project. It will be a battle for the explicit rejection of all forms of oppression, from whatever quarter they may come.

We do not seek to train pacifists—meek, adaptable souls, willing to live in peaceful coexistence with injustice without protest, without struggle, out of fear, convenience, or self-interest.

We seek to train *militants,* fighters for the kingdom, strugglers for justice.

Besides, we find that members of our CEBs are more in favor of a *peace born of justice* than of war or armed struggle. An armed struggle has never been provoked by those who live in the rural areas of this diocese. They have been marginalized their whole life long, trodden underfoot in their dignity by an oppressive class in control of the means of production and seeking all profit and advantage for itself. We want to do away with this class struggle, and we intend to be in the middle of it. It must be done away with from within. But we will not instigate it, nor will we stir up age-old sentiments of hatred, vengeance, and sadism, which have the power to motivate a deep-rooted, permanent struggle.

Further: we think that the rural workers of our area, the CEB members, ought to look for, and respect, the truth there is in others. That is, they ought to discover the truth held by their very oppressors, acknowledge it publicly, and trust that God has the power to convert the oppressors' hearts. We believe in the resurrection of all men and women, including oppressors. We reject no dialogue with sisters and brothers, nor do we refuse them our love. Our object is to help generate, in the hearts of the people, the same comradely openness toward the oppressors as there is in the heart of God. We beg for our oppressors, as for ourselves, the Lord's mercy.

To this end, a nonviolent struggle, taking its inspiration from the gospel, can be our struggle. We don't know how to wage it. How often we fall back into our old tradition, that of an all-out mentality of violence!

But we shall continue to encourage the humble practice of radical struggle for a change in society, rejecting all forms of repression, all forms of armed struggle, whatever their source, because such a struggle is always oppressive.

By "violence" I mean the use of force against the rights of the people. In particular circumstances, when the armed struggle of a whole people appears as the last resort against an oppressive tyranny, the nonviolent will take up arms along with everyone else, but they will refuse to abandon themselves to vengeance, torture, terrorism, or disrespect for the genuine rights of the conquered.

We are in disagreement with the forces of domination. Whenever society exploits the people of the countryside, we have the duty to disagree. And we disagree out loud, in an organized open manner. But in no way are we guerrillas, in no way do we seek an armed struggle. We condemn such a struggle, we disapprove of it, especially when its purpose is to maintain the unjust organization of society to the advantage of a small group and the disadvantage of everyone else.

11

THE CHURCH IN DIALOGUE

I have just spoken of the creation of conditions in which the people of the countryside and the outskirts of our cities may become militants in the battle for the kingdom of God and the battle for justice. And I have stipulated that the interior attitude, the attitude of heart, that must prevail in all of this must be inspired by the nonviolence of the gospel.

It is altogether to be expected that my readers will ask: Under the present political regime in Brazil (1981), and given the form in which the state assumes political and economic power here, what kind of dialogue does the church of Crateús envisage as possible, effective, and consistent with its loyalty to the gospel and the people?

In my view, this is a problem that, in its acute, nationwide form, we have rarely posed. We are still at the beginning of the road, still modestly in the "grade school" of political struggle. We are simply motivated by faith, inspired by faith. Faith is our "distant outlook."

Our initial practice, only a few years old now, does not give us a very broad view of the matter. Still, it will be possible, to my present way of thinking, to suggest certain reflections.

It would appear that, in the region of Crateús, as throughout the northeast and the whole of Brazil, the means of production and exchange are in the hands of a few. This vertical, pyramidal structure of Brazilian political society entails an assault on the dignity and basic human rights of the victims of oppressive marginalization: an immense multitude of Amerindians, landless *camponeses,* small farmers, farm hands, migrant workers, persons and families who live in the shadow of our great cities, the unemployed, the underemployed.

A member of any one of our Christian communities, upon discovering the discrepancy between his or her faith in human dignity and the national political project, cannot remain silent.

I have the impression that political power in Brazil, incarnate in the state, is more at the service of the economic and cultural elite than at the service of the great popular masses.

When a five-year plan is drawn up, when goals are selected, the words used appear to indicate priorities that will benefit the weakest. But in actuality these are projects of technocrats, who believe more in scientific technology than in the experience of the people. The people is marginalized when it comes to active participation in social development. Official planning betrays a radical diffidence in the people as the agents of its own history.

I call this established, institutionalized violence. It is not only practiced by economic forces, but protected by the political power of the state.

Faced with this situation as I see it, it is clear that *dialogue* will include, first, an attempt to make a lucid reading of Brazilian politico-economic reality. My aim is for the men and women of the countryside to have their eyes wide open, to be able to make use of a certain "critical lucidity." This is why I encourage the multiplication of base communities, CEBs, where these persons may meet, analyze the facts, and grow in critical awareness.

This is a necessary condition for dialogue. You can't have dialogue with your eyes closed. Dialogue must be entered into with lucidity, always.

A second condition will be that this reading done by the people of the countryside not be superficial. It must be a reading that goes to the root of established violence. It will presuppose, in the case of the people of the countryside, the collaboration of scholars and experts. All of the intelligentsia who believe in the people and its historical calling, who are disposed to respect the people and who wish to place their expertise at the service of this pilgrimage, are welcome among us, and we are most happy to have them.

Some theologians, technologists, and scientists have already come to Crateús, to help us reflect objectively on the causes of the present institutionalized situation of violence and oppression.

These experts provide the communities with a launching pad for their own perception, their own critical discernment, of any element of truth in the actions of those who hold economic and political power.

We have no wish to battle the might in a spirit of sectarianism. What we seek to combat in them is their responsibility for the structures and ideologies of oppression. We shall fight their objectively oppressive activity. We have no quarrel with their hearts, their basic rights, their dignity as human beings. We intend to respect these persons. They are human beings like anyone else. In this spirit, we hope to arrive eventually at an attitude of nonviolence that will look for truth in our adversaries, and, in dialogue with them, explicitly recognize their truth, even though with full knowledge that they are oppressors.

Some may judge this pedagogical approach too naive. But it is the basic attitude underlying our work. To be sure, this is not what the human heart seeks. We have a heart that is not only human, but brutish, and we should like to repay everyone "an eye for an eye."

Indeed, our lives transpire in an atmosphere where this mentality is all but universal—and this scale of values is instilled in us, day after day, moment after moment, by all the media—that violence must be repaid with violence. Our church groups, then, will have to discover, in their own practice, and in their reflection on this practice, a profound sense of gospel-inspired nonviolence.

So much for the conditions for dialogue.

Now, with this as our starting point, we intend to *require and demand,* along with the whole people, organized or organizing in the struggle for justice, that the economic and political powers lay down their instruments of oppression, dismantle their mechanism of exploitation of the lowly and the weak. As long as power-holders continue to reinforce their privileges at the apex of the sociopolitical pyramid and exploit the lowly and the weak, we cannot sit back, we cannot rest. The struggle must go on. And it is going to be a very long, all-embracing one.

It is in no way our intention that the means of production, along with wealth and culture, presently monopolized by the dominant classes, come to be monopolized by the oppressed classes. We seek the full participation in ownership, power, and knowledge—in *having, acting, and knowing*—of all persons who believe in human dignity and respect human rights. Only those are excluded who exercise domination and commit exploitation, and only insofar as they exercise domination and commit exploitation. The moment they have a change of heart and attitude, and try to dismantle the mechanisms of exploitation that they have been encouraging, and become our companions in the struggle for justice, they will be completely welcome.

Obviously, all that I am saying is like a mere whisper addressed, hand over mouth, to a global, challenging problem. We are too insignificant, out here in this hidden corner of Ceará.

But we are absolutely certain that, at the heart of our practice, in conjunction with the practice of the oppressed the world over, *all of this will come about.*

We consider that, in order to have dialogue, it will be necessary to be genuine and honest with political power—with the state. If we know that, through its projects, its investments, its policies, the state is favoring the interests of the dominant classes, and safeguarding their privileges, we cannot accept peaceful coexistence. We cannot undertake any kind of dialogue that would imply a legitimation of the established disorder. In these circumstances, dialogue will not include peaceful coexistence. Dialogue will require a ceaseless battle for a radical change of all the structures of oppression and exploitation.

Now, how will it be possible to reconcile, in the hearts of our people, this radical struggle for a change of structures that are the privilege of the great, with an interior attitude of nonviolence inspired by the gospel?

Practice alone will teach us. We shall try, gropingly. Not everyone in the world will be with us. If we observe the various classes—the intellectuals, the wealthy, the technologists, the politicians, and the popular classes of the entire world—we see that it is these last who are most inclined in their hearts to embrace an attitude of nonviolence.

And so in the popular milieu we shall find a great deal of cooperation for dialogue, and a synthesis between the attitude of radical struggle for justice and openness of heart to a recogntion of the truth in the hearts of others.

12

THE POLITICAL DIMENSION
OF FAITH

The long history of evangelization would seem to show that the church has never really come to grips with the political dimensions of pastoral ministry, faith, and the gospel.

When, in our evangelization, we hide something that the Lord has revealed, we are betraying the gospel in some way, however unconsciously. Now, it so happens that we find revealed in Jesus Christ, and proclaimed by the church as well, God's great proposal. It is a proposal made of God's free initiative, and is totally gratuitous. I must accept what the Lord grants me the grace to accomplish in an act of faith, if I am to accept it at all.

I am convinced that this proposal of God's has absolute priority. Faith tells me that the only project I have the right to accept is the Lord's project, the project of the living God who hears the cry of an oppressed people, who decides, irreversibly, to liberate them, and who calls the Moses-type leaders of all times to join together in a global strategy at the service of this people's liberation.

Political strategy, then—which is the key to the organized participation of the masses in this project of liberation—is part of the very intention of God, and at the root of our faith.

Our faith shows us a horizon. The God of Jesus Christ has summoned us not to pitch our tent once and for all in the carnival of history, but to build the future, gradually, within that history. It is in "transhistory" that we shall see the pitching of the everlasting

Tent, in which there will be no more tears in anyone's eyes because God will have dried them. This horizon mobilizes us for the continuous transcendence of all of the projects of today. When we build today, with passion and vigor, we are straining toward tomorrow.

All the political projects of today are limited and incomplete. They fail to exhaust, to incarnate totally, the project of God. And so the critical horizon furnished us by our faith enables us to participate in political life, steadfastly and in the thick of things, with open, loyal hearts—and yet to know that this is not the definitive solution.

There is more. Faith is a permanent light of critical discernment in the hearts of the people of the countryside. The light of faith shining in the base church communities makes it possible for Christians to examine their own attitudes, in order to discover whether these attitudes are consistent with the kingdom of God and the gospel, or whether they are inspired by oppression, hatred, revenge, or the will to power.

Faith has a basic contribution to make to political practice itself. Persons whose regard is superficial, who act on first impressions, and who say that what we are dealing with here is a "politicization of the faith" and a betrayal of the doctrine of the church, fail to understand the thinking in question.

To really get to know someone, as the saying goes, you have to "spend a month of Sundays" with that person. And so I invite all of our friends who do not understand us to come and spend a month of Sundays with us—to engage in the same practice and effort of discernment as we in a joint endeavor. Afterward they may tell us whether this is politicization of the faith or a dimension of faith revealed by the Lord—a question that many Christians leave in abeyance, unconsciously, perhaps, and innocently.

13

SPIRITUALITY OF THE SUFFERING SERVANT

The great masses of the oppressed, awakening to their mission, can find support and sustenance in the spirituality of the Suffering Servant.

I believe a great deal in the word of the Lord. I love to meditate on it. I love to let the Lord light up my life with his word. I have no very advanced exegetical or theological knowledge of that word in scripture. But as I see it, Second Isaiah placed a great deal of insistence on the Servant of Yahweh. And suffering is an important dimension of the picture of that Servant as it is presented to us. This is why so many have called him the Suffering Servant. The dimension of suffering, of *kenósis,* is intimately bound up with liberation and glorification. It, too, is a gift of the Lord.

In the hearts of our people we find the conviction that all who are crushed by injustice and violated in their dignity and rights, are equivalent to martyrs. They have great power of intercession before the Lord's throne.

If an example would be helpful, we might consider this one. A man was found beaten to death in the red-light district of Crateús. Near his grave today there is a little "pagan shrine," and lighted vigil lamps often appear there. There is evidently a popular belief in his power of redemptive mediation.

In the mind of the people, anyone dying from a drought, or ill-treatment, anyone executed at the hands of the law, stepchildren dying as a result of ill-treatment at the hands of their stepparents, and so on, are practically considered saints. It would seem that the masses see, in the very annihilation of victims of injustice, a power of mediation and redemption, which they intuit in mysterious, mystical fashion.

In the popular culture, many believe that, when one offers the Lord one's cross, that cross becomes liberative, and can help others. I should like to discover, validate, and encourage this experience of the cross—that of one's own cross, which, taken up with the cross of Jesus Christ, becomes a force for liberation. I consider this element of popular piety to be of great importance.

I am convinced that today's cross is a force for liberation today. It is not only the Lord's passion that is prolonged today in the flesh of our brothers and sisters, who are Jesus as Suffering Servant today. It is his liberation, as well, fully operative today, and destined to be consummated beyond history.

And so, I believe, we must encourage our crushed, suffering comrades to unite themselves to Christ on the cross, and to believe in the liberative force of their own cross.

The little group called "Friends of the Suffering Servant," who are looking for a more radical experience, can provide ongoing encouragement for a prophetic witness to be provided to the whole diocesan church.

14

POLITICAL PROJECTS
AND GOD'S PROJECT

To my way of thinking, the church of Crateús does not put forward—must not put forward, has no right to put forward—the blueprint for a new society. It has no right to present a political strategy for the implantation of any such project. It has no right to become the leader of the political community. It has no right to organize political society.

If it were to do so, little by little a new type of clericalism would return, one that would be worse than ever. In days gone by, clericalism was more or less unconscious. Today, the heightened consciousness of the church is incompatible with clericalism. Clericalism today would be theocracy. We live in an age of secularization, an age of the legitimate autonomy of "the world," not of the sacralization of politics. Theocracy must be rejected, for it is to society, and not to the church, that God has entrusted the guidance of the process of the development of the political community.

For all these reasons, the church must not furnish Crateús with a politico-historical project.

But I believe that the church does have the mission to animate and encourage, by way of the gospel, secular projects for society in Crateús. It is the task of the church to discern, in these projects, an openness to God's project. It is the task of the church to call to mind the horizon that should serve as the critical element in political practice, and to testify to the gospel throughout the process.

Any political project, *any* project for a society, inevitably either fosters human dignity, especially that of the very poorest, or else fosters disrespect for the human face of the daughters and sons of God. There is no neutrality here. It is the task of the church of Crateús, consequently, to exercise an ongoing critical vigilance in the analysis of all existing projects. The church will attempt to judge to what extent these projects contribute to the people's actualization of their calling in history and to others' respect for their basic rights and dignity—or, instead, to combination and oppressive marginalization.

We are indifferent to no political project. We must recognize all of them, and be present to them as Christians, as church, simply in virtue of the divine mission that the church has received from Jesus Christ. In the name of the faith, and with one eye on the reign of God, we must be present to all political projects.

It is the divine mission of the church in Crateús to assist Christians who commit themselves to anything in the political community—to help them be faithful to the people, faithful to the calling of the people, faithful to the rights of the people, faithful to God's project. But we must not lose sight of the horizon toward which we are journeying, remembering that concrete political projects are not the last word. They are all to be transcended.

In order for the people to be able to be faithful to this great project of God's, the church must be acquainted with political strategies, and must exercise in their regard, in conjunction and cooperation with the people, its mission of being light, salt, and leaven.

It is wrong to say, "This is the mission of the state. The church should stay in the sacristy." I totally and unequivocally reject a church of sacristies. When we physically close ourselves up in our sacristies, it is only in order to be present once more to the political community at the first opportunity.

From this viewpoint, we may say that the church in Crateús ought to be present to the entire political life of the country, its entire economic, cultural, administrative, and technological life, not with a partisan political presence, or a "technical" one, or one of active participation in the organization of society, but with a presence of watchfulness over the rights and dignity of the human person, and over God's project of justice, truth, and freedom.

Our outlook is ecclesial, derived from faith and revelation, and evangelical, and not one of partisan politics. We are not saying that the people ought not to take sides in politics. We hold that lay Christians should be involved with the political community, in accordance with the free option of their conscience. They should participate with loyalty and clear vision. The technical, strategic, partisan political perspective has great importance in the whole process of a project for society, and the laity should take an active interest in all of this.

The church of Crateús—the bishop, the priests, other pastoral ministers, the basic communities in their capacity as grassroots church—the church itself, has no right to direct local political society, or its economics, or its culture. But it has the right to be an animating, encouraging presence, in the name of God, in the name of the kingdom and the gospel. It has the right not to be excluded from anything at all, under any pretext. But its outlook is that of the gospel.

There are two vantage points for observing the same reality: the sacred and the secular. They are not irreconcilable, they are not mutually opposed, and they ought to be harmonized. Their alleged opposition is created by sectarianism or dogmatism on either side.

15

A SCHOOL OF LIFE

The reading primer *ABC da Emergência* ["ABCs for an emergency"] may look like political interference on the part of the church in official undertakings.

In 1980 the state of Ceará suffered an almost total drought. From March onward there was no more rain. Farm production fell to a minimum, and millions of families in the northeast of Brazil were hungry. In this situation the church had two alternatives. One was to have compassion on the misery of its children, our sisters and brothers victimized by the drought, and set up campaigns of aid and solidarity to wipe out their hunger. So many had done this in the past, so many are doing it today, and with the best intentions in the world. So many holy women and men had committed themselves along these lines, and we could have opted for this alternative.

The other alternative—the one we chose—was to profit from the experience of unions and communities. Their approach was to ask the hungry, "How are you faring with this drought? Are governmental emergency services doing any good? What have you proposed, or what are you proposing, to the government?"

Inasmuch as the means at the disposal of the unions and communities for putting together all the responses to these questions were more limited than our own, we offered our services for this purpose, and drew up a "primer," the *ABC da Emergência*. But it was the unions, and the base communities—the *camponeses* themselves—who had developed the content.

This being the case, it cannot be said that the official church—the bishops and clergy of Ceará—directed the process of the conscientization of the *camponeses* in this regard. Of course, in itself the conscientization of the *camponeses* within the church and in the light of the gospel would indeed be the mission of the church.

The question might be asked: What opportunities could the people possibly have had to discover, in this situation, what is called the "function of rebuilding a dismantled world"? How can one think of changing things when all the tools seem to be in the hands of those who exercise power?

The question is a challenging one, and we have not yet found, in Crateús, the complete answer. But here are the early beginnings of an answer.

I recall an experiment a preacher in the United States performed in a stadium one night. He arranged to have the lights go out once the stadium was full. Then, in total darkness, he lit a match. Suddenly there were other matches being lighted—and little by little, the whole stadium was illuminated. Then the preacher had the lights put back on and asked that the matches be put out. Now he made his point: "Better to light a match," he said, "than to spend all night complaining how dark it is."

I also remember a very popular and much-used parable. Once, in a little town in the interior of the country, there was a street. It was littered with rubble, packed with trash and rubbish. Every day the residents looked out of their windows and cried, "What a mess! And this messy street means nothing to the government, nothing to the mayor!" And the street got dirtier every day. Then one day a woman said, "You know what? I'm going to clean up the street in front of my house." And so she did, and it looked nice. Her neighbors then said, "You know what? We can do the same thing." And in no time the street was clean.

Moral: "If you want a clean street, clean up your part of it."

The members of our diocese are grasping this pedagogy more every moment, starting with their little local practice in their base communities. Their universe is here and now. By their local practice, and their collective reflection on it, they discover, and *actually experience,* their powers of creativity. That is, they begin little by little to occupy the space that belongs to them.

They learn to discuss, to plan, to make decisions, to team up for work in the field, and to recover, by law or by the sweat of their brows, what they have been robbed of. They learn to demand that the authorities respect their rights.

Through a transforming local practice, they gradually perceive their ability to change history, to change the universe. But this perception calls for a strategy, to be developed and shaped with a great deal of clear-sightedness and wisdom. The development of such a strategy is demanding, and may be a long-term affair. What is important for us is to keep lighting the matches, one by one, until the whole world is illuminated, beginning with that first match, beginning with a community that cleared up its own yard, beginning with a local struggle that has spread like wildfire.

Little deeds can shed a little light on difficult global questions.

In the interior of the diocese one day, we had a discussion with a group of farm workers about what we could see was the structured plundering of the region. We made a comparison with the rain that fell in the Jaguaribe river basin. The Jaguaribe had its source quite nearby, in a little stream called the Trici. During the winter the rains fill reservoirs, form underground lakes, fill some water holes and pools. But most of the water runs off and down to the sea, which has so much already!

Residents of the area were looking for a way to keep more of that water *at their service.* They were building reservoirs, dams, dikes, and irrigation canals.

The sweat of the brow of a *camponês,* we said, is like a great river. Owing to the mechanisms of commerce, the interplay of the "middlemen," and the activity of the financiers and banks, the sweat of the brow of the poor is almost all drawn off into the sea of the pockets of those who already have so much.

What is God's proposal here?

God has said, "With sweat on your brow shall you eat your bread."

In God's intention, the honest sweat of one's brow represents the human subsistence of the husband, the wife, and the family that depend on them. Whenever the mechanisms of commerce and production draw off a part of the honest sweat of the brows of the poor, to the profit of the dominant classes, we have formal disrespect for God's law, and public, organized sin. We have an assault on the dignity of our brother and sister, the laborer.

What should we do?

Not far from the place where we were holding our discussion, I was shown a waterhole. It had been dug with public funds—that is, with the people's money. (Public authority has no money. It comes from the people's sweat, to be managed for the good of all, especially the lowly and the weak.) The local town councillor had taken over the whole thing, fenced it off, built a gate, and restricted its use to the members of his political party. The members of the community held a meeting, and went to hold a dialogue with the councillor. They tried to reason with him. "Look," they said, "open it up, so everyone can come for water. The waterhole was dug with public funds, and is not supposed to be monopolized by an individual." The councillor refused. So the community said, "All right, we're all going to go there, pull down the fence, and post a watch so that everyone can get in and use the water."

And so they did! And everyone uses the water.

This example made it quite clear that it is possible to take back power that has been unjustly taken away. It is possible, without using violence—that is, without using force *against someone else's rights*—to repossess the use of one's own rights.

Thousands of little grassroots experiences like this one demonstrate the people's ability to organize its living space. Later on, these spaces can be joined together into broader areas—regional, national, and worldwide.

This hope I hold. But it is an obscure certitude. Only after human efforts turn it into experience does certitude become manifest.

16

SOCIALISM?

I have at present no data or methods for scientific proof of what I am about to tell you.

It would seem that those who have income in Brazilian society in the form of profits should be subjected to a sliding-scale tax for the good of all. The seventy to eighty million Brazilians who are too poor to maintain a decent human life would be exempt from this tax. In taxing the very poor, the treasury is usurping, to the advantage of the state as such, what belongs by basic right to the poor.

We know for a fact that a great many companies manipulate their accounts. They keep two sets of accounts, one for internal use, the other for tax purposes. There are a thousand ways of evading taxes, and the big corporations know them all. They even bribe the internal revenue agents.

Most Brazilians do not even make enough to buy food for themselves. When they are tempted to follow in the footsteps of the great, they do so so clumsily and by such naive means that they are easily caught. Then it's jail and, often enough, police brutality.

I'm convinced, then, that, in Brazilian society, the majority of the people—those who lack the bare necessities—ought not to have to pay taxes. Instead, profit-makers should have to pay a sliding-scale tax, for the common good. This would permit a certain redistribution of the national income, and help us come a little closer to a society of equal opportunity for all. It would be more just and equitable.

In the church of Crateús, then, we are combating the capitalist

economic model. What are we trying to do, then, implant a socialist model? Is the socialist model the only one we think capable of
solving our problems?

May the reader permit me to recall once more that my point of
departure is the outlook of faith, of the gospel, of the kingdom,
and not any technological or partisan political perspective.

From a point of view of faith, I believe that it has been revealed
by God that goods created *for everyone* are intended with absolute
priority *for everyone*. Individual appropriation must be subordina-
ted to this "universal destination of goods." If certain persons have
superfluities, they are only the administrators of those superfluities
for the common good, and have no right to use them simply
according to their own inclinations.

I repeat, the church has no plan for a political or economic
society. But—I also repeat—the church demands, in any proposal
for society, that this datum of revelation be incorporated: *the goods
of the earth are for all*. In other words, *all have a right to have, to
know, and to act.*

Now, an analysis of existing capitalistic projects shows that, even
when they are called neocapitalistic, or when they are more sophisticated forms of capitalism, they *fail to put bread for all on the
table of the banquet of life*. They concentrate on the table of the
great, to the grave prejudice of the masses. Historically, we cannot
hope that a capitalistic project will respect and incarnate the proposal of faith, of the kingdom, and of God.

Then does the church propose a socialistic alternative?

In Crateús, neither the diocese nor the CEBs have ever proposed
this.

We may have an opinion—a simple, personal opinion; everyone
has the right to an opinion. But we make no such proposal in the
name of our ecclesial mission. Nor does it seem to me that the
church of Brazil has made one.

We can, however, ask the following question. Might the broad
lines of socialism be able to harmonize with the demands of faith,
in a future undertaking to be developed by the whole Brazilian
people?

Not as a bishop, now, and not in the name of the experience of
the church of Crateús, I shall venture to propose my own view on
this question.

All existing socialist models are open to criticism. They are all imperfect and improvable. They neither fully incarnate God's project, nor do they attempt to do so—that is, to place at the disposition of *everyone* the opportunities that God wishes for *everyone*.

In so many socialist projects, a *party dictatorship* has created an internal oligarchy, which absorbs and usurps the decision-making power of the masses, and marginalizes them.

I see, then, no socialist model in the world today that the people of Brazil might copy. But at the same time I think that the broad lines of socialism—*ownership* for all, *knowledge* for all, *power* for all, and especially *decision-making power* for all—could well inspire a Brazilian political blueprint if the people, conscious and organized, so wishes it.

This *socialization of opportunities* is compatible, in my view, with the gospel, with God's intentions. It does not, however, exhaust the gospel. It is not the whole gospel.

17

CHRISTIAN FAITH AND MARXIST ANALYSIS?

For a political project incorporating socialization, does a Christian have a right to use a Marxist analysis of capitalistic society?

We stand at the beginning of a pedagogical experience. We have had only a twelve-year experience with base church community practice in Crateús. Any response to this question that I may give will be that of someone who is still searching, someone who does not yet see very clearly.

It seems to me that all the members of CEBs, and all Christians, must gradually learn to read reality with a double regard: a *human regard,* which some call "socio-analytic," and the *regard of faith.*

The human regard springs from human experience, human knowledge, human sciences. All the techniques and technologies, sciences and scientific tools of analysis, are welcome, regardless of their origin, if they help the people to an objective understanding of reality, and help the people actualize God's plan. I am not closed to any contribution, regardless of whose it is. Furthermore, I find that no genuine contribution can come from anywhere but the heart of God, the sole font of truth. God is praised and glorified when a human being, whoever he or she is, whatever his or her ideology, offers us a genuine scientific instrument for the analysis of reality.

The view of faith is a *free gift of God.* We cannot ask it of science or human reason. We can ask it only of the Lord, of the word, in contemplation, prayer, and the humble seeking of the heart.

These two views must be permanently interconnected in the practice of the people. We are trying to find the pathways of this articulation, this interconnection. To this purpose we analyze and debate the political projections of the government, and the structures and ideologies of society, and at the same time we read and meditate God's word, and seek to see reality with the *light* that comes as a free gift of God.

But I close no door to the scientific instrumentality that Marx offers us for an analysis of capitalist society simply because it comes from Marx. Whatever may be true in it is no longer from Marx but from humanity. I found it very interesting to be invited by a group of bishops to participate in a meeting on tools for the analysis of reality conducted by some theologians and some very competent social scientists. The course also helped us see what in "Marxism" comes from Marx and what comes from his disciples. It helped us read the Marxist projection—its scientific instrumentality for analysis, its materialistic conception of history, the dialectical method, and so on—in the light of the Christian faith.

I think that, in order to be honest with our Christian consciences, we must accept Marxist analysis and any other contribution human beings might make for a realistic analysis of our situation.

18

THE RELIGION OF THE PEOPLE

Does the religion of the people have any value for our plans for the church of Crateús, or for the plans for a society that the church of Crateús seeks to serve?

Living as I do with the priests, religious, and laity in the base church communities of Crateús, I am more and more convinced that the *intellectual world and the popular world are different worlds.*

The people has its own cultural, political, and religious *universe,* its history, ancestral memory, symbols, expressions, and language. We "intellectuals" have lost the key that could decode the message from the popular world.

There have been a few attempts, modest ones as yet, to build a bridge between the popular world and the intellectual world. These attempts have been looked on with suspicion in Brazil. And someone of the international stature of a Paulo Freire has been shunned as dangerous!

All our cultural and intellectual formation in the schools, especially in the universities, is totally divorced from any foundation in the people, and creates practically insuperable obstacles to any access to the popular universe. And then, incredibly, we consider that we have the right to interpret the people, lend the people our voice, speak in its name, and say what it is thinking!

We have no bridge to the religious universe of the people. Our europeanized theological training gives us few reading keys to the religious world of the poor, the world of popular piety. I find, for this reason, that we should very modestly recognize that we do not know the religious world of the people or its piety, and that we have no right to formulate theses on it, except as hypotheses to be verified and tested, patiently and at great length.

Our task is a search, with humble heart and clear head, and this means a long, open, and disarmed *common experience* with the people. As we gradually begin to learn something, we shall see that there is a solid deposit of popular *wisdom* there, and that it is a wisdom of many worlds at once. If we were to write wisdom literature today, there would not be just five or six books, as in the Bible, but dozens, sprung from the soil, the mind, and the consciousness of the people.

We have no means or criteria by which to recast the people's faith. We can only stammer, calling to the people from the outside, for we know only the surface, and we try to interpret without first understanding. And so I think that we shall have to make a further evaluation of all this common experience, as we live together with the people, we priests, religious, laity—and why not bishops? We should be willing to live with the people in silence, listen to the people for a long time, with the ears of the heart open, in order to grasp the popular religious world. This will allow us to "tune in on" the people, in a kind of spiritual symbiosis, so that we will be able to receive from the people the good news that comes from their life. And this will allow us to construct, tomorrow, a realistic theory of popular faith, popular piety.

Meanwhile, we grasp certain phenomena and expressions today. For example there has been importation and fraud. The religious consciousness of the people has absorbed, from the preaching of the missionaries, from the evangelization of the past certain values that are more cultural than religious. The people has translated theological theses, human theories, and religious slogans in its own way, and put them into practice.

And so we know that there is an expurgation, a purification, to be undertaken. But we have no rigorous criteria of discernment here.

We know, furthermore, that the church history of our country, the missionary enterprise, went hand in hand with the colonization enterprise. Colonization did not favor the people. It favored the dominant elite. The establishment of the first colonial provinces (the *capitanías),* the land grants, the great ranches and estates, all these were a great pie divided up by the papal government into Europe among its favorites. The fate of the Amerindians, the original landholders, was brutal decimation.

This being the historical reality, it is natural that the religious realm and the economico-political realm should be joined together in the mentality of the people. How could it be otherwise?

By the little glimmers that we have of the religious universe of the people it would appear that the people's *resistance* to colonization and neocolonization must be considered heroic. It is an expression of popular religion. Does this resistance reflect what theologians call a *sensus fidei,* a sense or instinct of faith, deeply rooted in the popular mind, telling it what is not faithful to the gospel? Surely this is a power of discernment that has served the people in history, and has enabled the people to save the church itself when a considerable part of the official church got off onto the wrong track.

In view of all of these considerations, I think that we have to live with the people and share its common experience. I think that we have to encourage ways of doing this. Not "insidious" ways, where intellectuals dress up like the hoi polloi and live among them in order to indoctrinate them. Nor with a "vanguard attitude," in order to do "research" at the grassroots level and then some political strategy planning without the people. This is a new form of what is called "populism"—another form of domination.

This common experience and common life should be geared to a long-term project, a project of listening, with head and heart, to the universe of the poor and its religious experience.

19

LIVING TOGETHER
AND LISTENING

For the first ten years of the history of our diocese, when I spoke of history, I spoke with absolute conviction of the people as *agent and protagonist* of this history, and I wanted to respect this, but I did not know how. I continually fell back into the old pedagogical habits that I carried about with me in my memory.

After the first ten years, I decided to give the grass roots back its *voz e vez*—"voice and vote"—in the pastoral process. We have been experimenting with this option for only five or six years now, and we do not yet have sufficient distance to make a value judgment. It may be several decades before such a judgment can be made.

In this second stage of the journey of our diocesan church, we are trying to hear the people more. There is a serious effort at listening. Those in charge of the diocese are continually invited to share in this experience, encouraged to do so, and encouraged to make a self-evaluation of their progress. I believe that we are making progress. We are growing. But the people's universe is still unfamiliar to us. We have but few basic criteria for exercising discernment in its regard. But we are trying very hard, in conjunction with other dioceses throughout the country.

I can cite an example from my personal experience. In the old days, the natural thing to do, before a pastoral visitation, was for the bishop to work out a plan with his advisors and make it known to the communities. The communities would be expected to follow a plan drawn up on the outside. The pastor would find various persons to help him carry out the program as it had been outlined. The faithful would come from afar to hear the long sermons of the missionaries and their bishop.

When, a few years ago, God gave me the grace to discover that the bishop had to be evangelized by the people, too, and that the people had an experience of the gospel to share with me for my personal conversion, I made an effort at listening. I remember a parish where I had gone to spend a month in pastoral visitation, visiting the communities. There was a kind of tension in all the communities. The *camponeses* would say, "We want to hear His Excellency. We have come to hear the Bishop. Lord Bishop, is His Excellency not going to speak?" And I would say, "I've come to *hear you!*"

Many a time I sat on the floor listening to their discussion, jotting down whatever I thought I might be able to use. Very rarely would I intervene. I would give only very short sermons, and I would always base them on what the people had experienced or said on the subject.

This experiment was very helpful to me. I was criticized, even by priests who loved the people very much. They considered me remiss in my duty. They would tell me, "The people have come to hear you and want to hear you. They say they want to hear what the bishop has to say."

I feel I should do much more listening. As the people takes up an active role, a harmonious mixture of the people's contribution and the bishop's contribution comes into being. Instead of the people always listening and the bishop always speaking—or vice versa—we are on the threshold of a synthesis, which will be in the form of a dialogue or a dialectic.

20

SPIRITUALITY AND POLITICS

There are two tendencies in the diocese of Crateús. There are those who emphasize spirituality, and there are those who emphasize the political dimension.

How may these two emphases be reconciled?

Saint Paul, it would appear, placed a great deal of emphasis on the inexhaustible wealth of the Spirit, who multiplies gifts with such great diversity. None of these gifts is the "total gift." The *gifts* of the Spirit must be harmonized, for the good of the whole church, the whole people.

This is what we find in Crateús. There is a variety of gifts of the Spirit. There is the gift of contemplation in the life of the people. Those who receive this gift feel that in their lives and their popular pedagogy they should concentrate on *the discovery of the living God* in the midst of the people: on the discovery of a liberator God, a God who prolongs the passion of Jesus in the flesh of the people, a God who wills the conversion of the people's hearts.

I call this dimension the "mystical" one. It is the contemplation of the Mystery of God as God is actually experienced in human lives, and I consider it of the highest importance. The diocese of Crateús needs it. I am grateful to God for having awakened this vocation in various persons of the church of Crateús— for having granted them this charism.

At the same time, there are many persons who discover—also by God's grace, also by the light of the Spirit, by a charism—that faith, religious practice, pastoral theory and practice, the church, the gospel, all have a political dimension, which we cannot hide, and which, most importantly, is a special revelation of God for our times. It is a dimension that has been far too little appreciated in past centuries.

These persons speak of this dimension with vigor and conviction. They put the accent on the pedagogy of the political dimension of faith. They are an inestimable contribution, then, to the future of the diocese.

The local church must harmonize the charism of contemplation and the experience of God with the charism of the political dimension of faith. The local church will be maimed, imperfect, incomplete, unless it synthesizes and integrates both dimensions.

All of us are imperfect and incomplete. It is easy, then, in a way, for either side to absolutize its position, to become "sectarian" about it. Those who have discovered the political dimension of faith consider the "mystics" the contemplatives, "alienated." Those who emphasize contemplation think that the "other side" is engaged in an "exaggerated activism," and a "politicization of the faith."

There can be passionate, sectarian moments, then, on either side. In the midst of these tensions, though, the Spirit invites us to a receptive openness and a change of heart.

I think that the bishop, having as he does the mission in his church of "strengthening his sisters and brothers in the faith," the mission of gathering together the various charisms for the unity of the whole, therefore has the task of harmonizing these two tendencies, encouraging the growth of each of them, and of seeing that they complement one another. This is not easy for me to do.

Some steps have been taken. For example, when the Friends of the Suffering Servant meet, they make it a point to bring up the political dimension. When the political dimension is discussed by Christian activists, they try to make sure that they include consideration of contemplative experience.

We are all called to conversion and openness, in both of these dimensions. We have tried, but we do not know how to go about it. There have been moments of difficult tension. These tensions have diminished now. Other, greater tensions will arise tomorrow, inevitably. But I am certain that, in the midst of all this, the bishop must become the one to gather up the various charisms, and along with his people, harmonize them for the common good of the church.

21

THE RADICAL GOSPEL

It seems to me that the basic experience in the church of Crateús is the experience of the radicality of the gospel, in a poor, simple common life with the people.

The first experience I had of this followed the arrival of Father "Alfredinho"—Frédy Kunz. He came to Crateús in 1968, dressed in the poorest clothing, without any knowledge of Portuguese, looking for experience with the very poorest. The bishop's residence wasn't the place. The poor were welcome there, but they came for alms or advice. That wasn't Frédy's place.

The house where a team of priests lived in a poor neighborhood was frequented by the poor. But not by the very poor. That wasn't Frédy's place.

One day Frédy was called to the bedside of an impoverished prostitute dying of cancer. She was mere skin and bones. Her name was Antonieta. By a God-given intuition, as he was sitting there, Frédy suddenly saw that this neighborhood of the most abandoned prostitutes was his place. He came to me to discuss the possibility. It seemed to me that the notion was from the Spirit, and that I ought to accept it. A good part of the clergy agreed. But some did not. "Impossible! Scandal!" And they suggested Frédy live in a house downtown, so that there wouldn't be the scandal of a priest living in the most sordid red-light district of the city.

Once he had been assigned there, some well-meaning lay persons came to me to ask me to take him out of the red-light district. It was a scandal, they said. My answer was, "Who will guarantee me that this call isn't from the Spirit? If it's from the Spirit, who's to say it's wrong?"

He stayed there for two years. Working in this sordid red-light district, Father Alfredinho discovered *a shrine of God.* When he told me about it for the first time, in his little adobe hut, it was hard to believe him. Theoretically I believed him. But I had been working so long with my moralizing mentality that it was hard to see things with his eyes. I asked him to jot down his discoveries and insights. Father José Bouchaud, superior general of the Sons of Charity, Father Frédy's order, published these notes of Frédy's in France, under the title, *L'ânesse de Balaam,* "Balaam's Ass."

On the very eve of its publication in Brazil, the book was judged to be subversive. But the director of Edições Loyola soon undertook to publish it and distribute it through the country. It also appeared in other languages.

Father Frédy's experience in the red-light district of Crateús was a profound shock to all of us. We saw that we had no right to judge others, moralize. We should have looked into the depths of the human heart, where the living God is present. And the living God is indeed present in hearts, liberating, sanctifying, and raising from the dead, in our very day. There is no limit to the liberative activity of God.

Frédy sought to live a radical poverty, as God had asked of him. Still, at first, he accepted help from charitable women, friends of his, in the form of money. Then, discreetly, he made small loans to one or other of the very poor. At once the word got around. And he was besieged with requests for loans. His image had been transformed into that of a good-hearted rich person, instead of a brother and comrade in the common experience of poverty. His sharing of the life of the very poorest looked entirely different now. From that moment on he refused to give anyone any money. In his adobe hut, the same one Antonieta had lived in until her death, he had only the bare necessities. He lived with his sisters the prostitutes in the simplicity of a beloved brother.

He continued the radical-gospel experiment in Tauá, where he was pastor. He did use the rectory, in the middle of town near the church, for his office. But his residence was a room in a broken-down hotel in a poor section of the town.

During a meeting with the Christians of Tauá, he heard strong objections. "Father lives in a hovel. He should live in the rectory. It would be more dignified."

Father Frédy asked, "Do you know the prefect of the city of Tauá?"

"Of course. Dr. Domingos."

"And where does he live?"

"He works in the prefecture and lives in his own house."

"Well, that's what I do. I work in the rectory, I receive you there, and I live in my little house. Will you deny me the right to choose where to live?"

After his term as pastor he went to live in Barra do Venta, in Serra de São Domingos, a village of some fourteen houses. He was installed in the ramshackle adobe shanty where maize was stored. But the families there were so attached to him that they decided to plaster and whitewash it. Then, teaming up, they built another building, which they named "House of Prayer and Defense of Human Rights." And they often met there for prayer and meditation. Everything was simple and poor.

In his long stay there, sharing the life and experience of the people, Father Frédy discovered the poorest of the *camponeses* to be an extension of the Suffering Servant of Yahweh. He decided to recount his experience in a book called "Uriah's Ewe," which presents the testimony of several of today's suffering servants— liberators unbeknownst even to themselves.

Father Frédy's experiment is an unending challenge to all of us in the diocese. He is fragile like the rest of us, a prodigal like the rest of us. But he wants to make a more radical response to the living God. And in doing so, he invites us, whose responses are comfortable, mediocre ones, to continual renewal.

I should like to mention another experiment, that of Father Eliésio dos Santos. The son of a poor railroad worker in Fortaleza, he earned his degree in the School of Geography and History at the Federal University of Ceará. He could have had a good job, with middle-class status, and helped his needy family. But he chose the interior. In Crateús, he worked as a teacher, earning little, living in a modest house open to all comers, and spending his free time in the pastoral ministry. In 1973 he was arrested with other pastoral ministers in the town of Poranga while engaged in giving a training course in evangelization to the people of the countryside.

He had made the socio-analytic comparison of today's society with a tree whose roots are thirsting for nourishment. The nourishment (wealth) is concentrated in the hands of a few. The fruit of the tree is rotten, and consists in injustice, exploitation, and so on. This tree was sketched on a poster and affixed to a wall. The Federal Police were informed, and they arrested the group as terrorists and hauled them off to Fortaleza. The Federal Police looked on the poster as evidence of a subversive plan worked out by the bishop of the diocese and executed by propagandizing agitators. The base church communities were alleged to be terrorist cells!

Eliésio's prison experience confirmed him in his desire to become a priest. He enrolled at the Theological Institute of Recife, living with a group of young men from various dioceses in Olinda. They were good, devout kids, but they felt no commitment to the people, and even got "fed up with hearing so much about 'the people.' " And Eliésio thought, "I can't live here."

I arranged with the seminary administration to have him live in Nova Descoberta, a Recife shantytown, with a team of priests and nuns, very close to the people. That was a very useful year for Eliésio, and gave him the grassroots experience of living with the very poorest.

But at the end of the year he told me, "Two more years and I'll be ordained. I'm learning to be the pastor in the outskirts of a big city. But my actual work is going to be with the *camponeses*. This isn't the right place for me."

I agreed to let him live in the Crateús region with Father Frédy, in Barra do Vento. He lived there as a field hand, working on the plantations, joining in the celebrations, visiting the *camponeses* in their houses. As he spoke with them and listened to them, he was assimilating the basic lines of the religious world of the people, and developing a theological reflection on the people. He was sketching a kind of pastoral response to the problems that he was discovering. A team from the theologate took care of the periodic supervision of his theological training.

Two years later Eliésio was ordained a priest. And today he is still a person who prefers the poor, a person for whom the poor have a special meaning.

A third experience is that of Abigail Reis. She was a Little Sister of Jesus, a disciple of Brother Charles de Foucauld. And her heart is still faithful to this inspiration and this charism.

She came to the diocese of Crateús, spent a year with Father Frédy and Eliésio in Barra do Vento, then switched to the mother church of São Gonçalo in Serra dos Cocos, living in the same poverty as the people. She fattened a pig, sold it, and bought an adobe hut. She furnished the place herself, plastered it, and fixed it up as a simple house of hospitality. And there she lives, earning her upkeep by baking banana and cocoa biscuits to sell, making artifacts, or planting some maize, potatoes, and bananas, all by herself.

And so she goes on leading the modest, simple life of the villagers, winning their friendship, sharing their prayer life, without exercising any direct leadership. She lets local leaders do their own jobs.

This is a testimony of great importance, especially for the mother church, São Gonçalo, where the diocese had granted fourteen parcels of land, belonging to São Gonçalo from time immemorial, to 160 families. The families organized the "Central Farm Cooperative," which retained ownership of the land, leaving each family the usufruct of its own plot. With outside money, the diocese hired professionals to take care of community education and train persons in co-op management.

Twenty-five mini-projects were set up. Every one of them failed!

That was when Abigail came on the scene—without any money, without advanced technical degrees, and without directing anything. She simply lived with the co-op members and welcomed them the way a sister would.

This testimony of Abigail was a challenge to the whole people, the whole church. It showed everyone the other face of what they had thought the church was—rich, with money to invest and pay for professional help in its various undertakings.

22

CONCLUSION

Now that I have come to the end of my testimonial, I wish to restate my intention.

In Latin America we witness a phenomenon deserving of a great deal of attention: the birth of a new face of the church, springing from the very life of the people by the power of God.

A number of Christians—lay, religious, priests, and bishops—feel called to engage in a pastoral practice that welcomes this new phenomenon.

We in Crateús feel called. I feel called as bishop of Crateús.

I doubt whether any of us has a definitive word to say.

We are all searching.

Inasmuch as we are all searching along somewhat different routes, with somewhat different pedagogical approaches, it seems useful for some of our sisters and brothers to make their experiences known, not as a model for someone else to copy, not as the last word, but as a way in which the church of Crateús is carrying on its search.

This has been my main intent in recounting something of this long history, which of course could not all be told in a few pages.

Only God can evaluate it in its totality.

I wish to leave all my brothers and sisters—the bishops, priests and lay persons who read this, if they have the patience to read it to the end—a request, a brotherly appeal.

Put your experience, your witness, down on paper.

I know that many of my brothers and sisters have had deeper, or at least broader, experiences than mine.

And I feel that I can ask *my sisters and brothers, the theologians,* to pore over all of this pastoral testimony, which will have been drawn up spontaneously, without the restraints of systematic reflection, and try to plumb the underlying models of church, to tell us to what extent they incarnate what is most fluid and promising for Catholic theology.

The complementary contribution of theologians will be indispensable.

I think that we are coming closer and closer to a *harmonization of the contributions of pastors and theologians,* in such wise that both together, joining their charisms and diverse talents, may be able to build a renewed Latin American church for tomorrow.

I wish to address a special appeal to *all who work with the people,* begging them to create a space in which the people can express its religious experience, communicate its faith, practice and formulate its pastoral activity and theory, and tell us, in its own words and style, how it visualizes this church that will be so much closer to the people.

These experiences on the part of the people must spread out and multiply. Publishers have brought out thousands of books written by intellectuals. But intellectuals are a minority of the population of the whole country. The great masses have a solid experience to report, a piece of good news to proclaim. If we give the people, or restore to the people, this same opportunity, we shall have a body of popular literary expression tomorrow.

The people of today has a wisdom that is often underestimated. We rob the people of its space in the organization of society, where it could develop and perfect the literary expression of popular culture.

Tomorrow, without becoming "intellectuals," the people, faithful to popular culture, will be able to express its perspective, its analysis of the more committed churches, and beautifully.

I end my testimonial with a cry to the four corners of the earth— a cry of hope that we will be witnesses of this new face of the church of Jesus Christ.

PART THREE

THE WITNESS OF CO-WORKERS

Bishop Fragoso sent copies of parts 1 and 2 of this book to pastoral co-workers in the diocese of Crateús. He asked them to put into writing their experience of the journey of the church of Crateús, their impressions of the emerging face of a church of the people, their witness.

Part 3 consists of some responses to that call. Because one of the main thrusts of Bishop Fragoso's work is to turn the "pyramid of power" upside down—to move the center of power in the diocese from the bishop to the priests and sisters, to the laity, to the poor—it is helpful to hear the voices of those who work at the periphery and who live and work among the poorest of the poor in Crateús.

Bishop Fragoso does not wish to be the only one to tell the story of the church in Crateús. Here others tell the story from their perspective. The statements give readers a view of the successes, failures, and hopes of those who are working to build a church of the poor.

1

HOW I SEE OUR DIOCESAN CHURCH

Paco (Father Francisco Almanara, S.J.),
*Priest-*campon\u00eas *in the Vicinity of Macambira*

Before I begin, it will be well to mention:

1. I've been two and a half years in the local church of Crate\u00fas.

2. My view of the diocese has been conceived from where I am in residence—in a place where communication is difficult, and where it's possible to know and feel what's going on in other communities and with other persons of the diocese only after a time lapse, and only indirectly and partially.

3 What I'm writing is more a start than a finished summary.

4. What I'm writing is not so much how I *feel* about the diocese, as it is how I *see* the diocese as a whole. (I'm trying to be more objective than subjective.)

5. I'm writing for you, the pastoral ministers of this diocese.

A SUFFERING CHURCH

Our local church of Crate\u00fas seems to me to be a suffering church:

1. It suffers because it is the people, and the people is a suffering people.

By this I mean that the active participation of Christians in pastoral planning, evangelization, evaluations, decisions, works, and the like, is becoming a reality, although we still have a way to go. This is occurring through the base-level communities—the most significant characteristic of the diocese—and other means (Pastoral Council, Administrative Council, CPT, and so on).

And as this people suffers—materially and nonmaterially—our church suffers too.

2. Our diocesan church suffers because it is a church coming to be, every day, emerging from the people, continually coming into being and being converted.

This effort, this conversion, is a long, endless journey, for pastoral ministers as well as for the people, because both are used to and comfortable with a past in which the church was traditionalistic, clerical, in the extreme.

Facts that prove this: The diocese is detaching itself from its "works." These are being given back to the communities, to individuals, to the people, more and more every day. Self-criticism (more or less prompt) is ongoing, so that our church may actually be a church of the people. The Pastoral Council is examining itself in these terms, and the recommendations for a future "meeting of the communities" and a "grand assembly" are likewise in this spirit. A real participation on the part of the people, the grass roots, in the work of the pastoral teams is being striven for. The main objective of the diocese this year is land distribution and rural ministry. And I could go on.

3. Our church also suffers because it is poor in leaders (quantitatively) to serve, further, and articulate means and ends along the common journey. It is also poor in material resources.

Local Christians demand this service and this help, and they are right to do so from where they are in their awareness. And we pastoral ministers would like to respond to this demand. But the task is just too big for us. I won't stop to mention any examples that we all face in all of the parishes, but just to take one example from a particular region, I especially feel this suffering in the area of Serra-Macambira, where we've practically given up on pastoral assistance. Because leaders are scarce in the diocese, we tend to favor regions and communities where work, the journey, is further along, and where our efforts are more likely to bear fruit.

Then there's the lack of resources. We've made an option for nondependence on economic help from the outside as a greater value, and we journey in this direction, which in a way limits us and in a way liberates us. But I find in the balance that it's the right option, because even the limitations have the effect of stripping us of privileges that lay persons don't have, and force us to share something of the insecurity in which they live their whole lives.

This is real solidarity. The church is turning more toward the people.

4. We are a church that feels a bit at sea sometimes, too, because we aren't always able to detect and celebrate points of convergence, the elements that unite us across our divergencies, across the elements separating us (which are also real).

5. I see our diocesan church as a church that *struggles* because it hopes and loves. I see communities more enlightened, and organizing; farmers really battling for their land, and managing to get free unions (Tauá, Parambu); persons gradually getting over their fear and believing in their own strength when they are enlightened and organized—when they are united; pastoral ministers helping and supporting the little ones, and right at their side. All this is because we hope and believe that the liberation the Father wills for all will come through this struggle.

6. The people is not vengeful. It seeks an egalitarian, just world for all (bosses too). And work groups (for instance, the CPT) have discovered that it is only by a struggle for true agrarian reform that the communion of fellowship already present in the hearts of the people and in the communities will come nearer to realization for all.

So many pastoral ministers really like the farmers and their families, with all their heart and soul. They pulsate with their small victories, weep with their sufferings and setbacks, and feel and show a holy wrath at the hardness of heart of the great, and zeal for the people God loves.

7. I see our church as a church on the road. This diocese has a clear preferential option for the people, the little ones, and a common pastoral approach (more or less well defined) that aims at the people's taking charge of the church itself and—as people and

as church—transforming reality and liberating itself from slavery.

True, there are different concrete ways of implementing this approach, and a diversity of ideals, personalities, habits of manner and action—but there is a unity shining through it all (perhaps more visible to those on the outside than to ourselves).

8. The church of Crateús is not at ease, is not comfortable. As a general rule it is open to self-questioning and open to questioning from the outside (for instance in the Pastoral Council, which is willing to evaluate itself and to be evaluated by persons on the outside). True, it is painful at times for all of us when we become aware of certain problems, and take them up and face them without losing our place, our identity, our confidence (pastoral ministers, priests, and others).

9. Until a little over a year ago, something else was beginning to unsettle us and confuse us (confuse the pastoral ministers, to the detriment of the people). Certain individuals, disaffected and angry, refusing to see the positive side of anything, closed and secretive, became prejudiced, formed cliques and little factions, and lost sight of a joint pastoral approach in view of the good of all.

I feel that all this is considerably improved now, and it seems that we were helped by the visit of Clodovis and Libânio, among other things. Maybe what we had to do was become more open and free, more realistic, and have a more consistent view of situations and ministries. I feel that the atmosphere isn't so charged now, we're more relaxed, and we can tell the truth and share our concerns and truly journey together by so doing.

10. I see our church of Crateús as a church *blessed by gifts of the Spirit,* and able to celebrate these gifts and be glad in them. I see so many individuals, among the people and the clergy alike, with so many dissimilar (thank God) human qualities and habits of action, so many persons placing their talents and ways of doing things (their charisms) at the service of their most abandoned brothers and sisters.

And we are trying to join these gifts together, as gifts of the Spirit, which cannot be mutually exclusive or noncomplementary. As I see it, we have made progress here, on the personal level (by individual effort) as well as on the diocesan level (for instance, coordination, parishes grouped by areas, an exchange of personnel for the sake of cooperation and sharing among all the parishes).

11. I also feel that we have learned a little better to rejoice together and celebrate this wealth of gifts (showered on us by God), and this interconnection among them, which, although slight so far, is growing (in our assemblies, processions, meetings, our Pentecosts—even with some still absent).

SOME DIFFICULTIES

There are difficulties in our church, and they act as a brake to this journey of ours—which is really progressing, but could always progress further and better. Here are some things that come to mind:

1. On the personal level: We've made progress here too, but there still are cliques and prejudices. We aren't objective enough to see the charisms and wealth of others, we aren't open enough to expect anything new in the life and work of "certain persons." We naturally tend to shut ourselves up in our personal pastoral views and think that others ought to "shape up or ship out." This sometimes prevents us from respecting others' levels of consciousness, from letting them walk at their own pace. It keeps us closed up and unable to question ourselves, unable to enrich one another and help one another make progress.

2. Similarly, it seems that we sometimes don't like to *look lovingly on the work of others,* their way of doing things, or even look lovingly on these individuals themselves. We'd rather ignore them or criticize them behind their back than rejoice with them and take a step forward.

To help us get over this, it would be a good idea to *communicate to others* what we ourselves are doing as individuals, what is going on in our movements, our meetings, and our parishes (as the CPT does, and, recently, the Movement for Nonviolence or Steadfast Resolve, as well as the Friends of the Suffering Servant, some parishes, and some individuals). The better we get to know one another the better we will be able to love and complete one another.

3. Less than before, but still a little, we see a certain *anticlericalism* among our ministers (lay, religious, and priestly). For example, we still occasionally ridicule individuals and their traditional attitudes, underestimate the value of the sacramental ministry, entertain an aversion for a particular priest or brother,

engage in whispering and backbiting that isn't constructive.

This sometimes confuses the people, on its particular level of consciousness, and can destroy this consciousness instead of helping it develop.

We don't face up to this anticlericalism (sometimes more emotional than rational) and come right out and talk about it with one another. If we allow this to continue, it may finally do away with the service, the role, of the priest and brother, which is a great "mystical" force among the people in its religious tradition, a force that can and should be a unifying and conscientizing element for the growth of the communities.

4. We have still not created a space for self-knowledge on the part of each individual—a way of knowing something more about what is going on within each of us from a *psychological* viewpoint—either because of our faults, our mood-changes, our prejudices, our lack of objectivity, and the way we distort reality— or because of our difficulties with adult relationships, our traumas and scars past and present—or because of our inability to believe that what happens in the future depends on us, regardless of what may have happened in our past.

5. Another difficulty, especially in some of our ministers, is a certain pessimism or *defeatism,* a notion that no progress is being made, while failing to be creative and open enough to propose a concrete, real solution and work together to achieve it.

Basically I think that sometimes we don't have the courage to accept our weaknesses and limitations, and so we settle for negative, uncreative criticism.

6. Sometimes too there is a difficulty with our *refusal to accept decisions made by democratic vote.* That is, some of our democratic decisions (on the Pastoral Council, in meetings, and so on) are not accepted by all of us, perhaps because we are not yet accustomed to thinking and living democratically, or because we are basically dictators.

For example, I think that when the majority decides on something—even when I've voted against it—I should accept this decision and work to carry it out (unless it's something seriously against my conscience).

I wonder whether this is why, right after we've decided on something, before giving it time or setting up conditions for carrying it out, before testing it, we turn around and change plans and decide something else.

7. Perhaps due to the quantitative poverty of our leadership, there is the danger that some communities (regions or groups) may get "too far ahead" (in organization, consciousness), owing to more help from the leaders, leaving behind and *forgetting other communities* (regions or groups) that are practically cut off or isolated because they are geographically remote to begin with, and have only begun the journey, so that they can't keep pace.

The result is the death of these communities or a wrong direction, leaving them worse off than before they began to be a community.

8. Another area in which we've made progress, but which is difficult (and will continue to be), is the *interconnection between the spiritual and the political,* between mystique and action, contemplation and practice, faith and life, with individuals, communities, groups (or movements), leaders, and the whole diocese.

In general I can say that each of us, with each one's individual charism, leans a little more to one side (the spiritual, explicit prayer, loving relationships, gratuity) or the other (politics, action, organization, efficiency), even though we try to interconnect both in our personal and community life.

I think that it really is important and essential for each of us to keep trying to lean in the opposite direction. If everyone defends and prioritizes his or her own inclination, we shall not succeed in interconnecting these two aspects of one and the same life, either in ourselves as individuals or in the whole diocese.

STRUCTURES AND MOVEMENTS

1. *Diocesan Pastoral Council.* The Pastoral Council as a coordinating and decision-making organ, with participation at the base-level (replacing the old clergy council), is an important step toward a new, popular church.

It is a good idea to handle one main subject in each council meeting, as we have been doing lately, instead of many, as before.

On the other hand, some of the matters treated seem not to be followed up, as if the council had exhausted the subject.

Decisions made at the last minute for lack of time, when we're tired and working too quickly, have negative consequences. Sometimes participants are walked on, and sometimes what is decided isn't accepted or acted on.

In openness and a spirit of self-criticism, we ought to admit that we haven't achieved a real participation on the part of the grass roots, and therefore need to come up with something new.

2. *Diocesan Administrative Council.* Planning and budgeting together with the people, with everything out in the open, with accounts made public, is no easy matter for a traditional, autocratic church. This is a very concrete step in this journey of ours toward a new church.

I support any effort to resolve the problem of church estates that tends to favor the very poorest by giving them these estates (to whatever extent this is possible).

I likewise support any effort of conscientization in the direction of an eventual abolition of stipends in connection with the sacraments, as we have already done with the Mass and confirmation.

3. *Coordination.* This is an effort on the part of the diocese to interconnect our activities, arising from a felt need (at least on the part of pastoral ministers!).

We are on the way to clarifying our objective and making it more concrete and efficient.

4. *Parishes.* The traditional structure is giving way to the new ecclesial practice—base-level communities, team ministry, and interconnection and coordination.

The interconnection of various parishes with one another in pastoral endeavors is a real help, a first step along the path of evangelical sharing.

5. *Vocations ministry.* I find this to be an essential initiative in this new church born of the people, something to be fostered very seriously and accepted by all (which is not quite yet the case, it seems to me). The way that this is being done from a point of departure in the concrete situation of the communities, in the light of deep reflection on the gospel, is, I find, the right way to discover the service God asks of each member of the diocese.

6. *CPT.* This is a central organization in the diocese. There is a danger it may become elitist, neglecting individuals or localities whose level of awareness is still very rudimentary. (This is only my opinion, and has only the value of an opinion offered by someone

who has not yet participated in any of the meetings because he feels that his own awareness is still far short of the level maintained by the community in which he lives.)

7. *Nonviolence and Suffering Servant Movements.* These are important for the diocese as a whole—more for the meaning of the struggle in the light of faith than as new organizations in addition to the ones already in place.

I find that both need to be better known and accepted (which will require an effort on the part of the members of these movements and those who are unfamiliar with them).

8. *Holy Childhood Movement.* This is clearly a movement in the spirit of the gospel. I think that it ought to continue to move toward being taken over—in the not too distant future—by the older girls themselves.

9. *Courses of study.* In principle these are necessary and good. But it seems to me that they are a luxury we can't afford. The return is too slight, as far as I can see. Perhaps we might be able to get along with fewer lecturers from outside the diocese, and ask them to stay longer instead. We might ask lecturers, with their own personality and approach, to cover a variety of topics. Then too we could perhaps take advantage of the hidden talents of our own diocese.

I see these courses as a need not accepted by all, and perhaps this is the main reason why they become a luxury with so little to show for it.

EMPHASES IN NEED OF COORDINATION

Looking at the diocese objectively—at the Christians of the communities, the pastoral ministers, the movements—it seems to me there are certainly a great many more elements of unity than of divergency or discord. But it is not always easy to "get into" this experience and perception of unity without being impressed by the aspects of divergency. If I'm not mistaken, this is a point on which we ought (at least sometimes) to be more realistic.

The more we can get over difficulties, the less our church will feel at sea, and the more strength we will have to struggle and forge ahead.

Our option is clear at the diocesan level, but it would be well to make the objective of the diocese more concretely explicit—something that I think would be more feasible now from a point of departure in parish objectives.

It's clear to me that:

1. The emphasis (by some of our ministers) on the mystico-evangelical, contemplative side, on loving relationships and gratuity, more imitation of Jesus' thirty years of hidden life, should not be allowed to be the main emphasis of the diocese. It needs a "political connection."

2. The emphasis (again, by some of our ministers, fewer this time) on explanation, on (scientific or theological) theory, intellectual conscientization, even from a starting point in the problematic of the people through a common lived experience with the people, is terribly dangerous if it neglects organization and concrete means, because it arouses persons for the struggle without giving them suitable weapons with which to wage the struggle.

3. The emphasis (by some of our ministers) on the politico-evangelical, active side, on organization and effectiveness, more in imitation of Jesus' public life, if disconnected from the other attitudes just cited, tends to fall victim to elitism or naivety, tends to lose its root strength, the horizon of its hope, its point of Christian and ecclesial reference, and the deep meaning of the struggle.

And so, without all three of these points or emphases together, our pilgrimage, our journey in this particular church will be short-lived. The basic attitude of the diocese must be the interconnection of all three. If we hope to journey at all, I think that each of us will have to try to connect, within ourselves, all three attitudes, while of course placing more emphasis on one of them, and will have to try to feel the wealth of others by openly accepting those who emphasize one of the others instead of our own.

Either we believe and feel that we complete one another, or we lose our chance to keep being, day by day, the new church born of the people.

2

EVALUATION OF OUR PRACTICUM IN CRATEÚS

Seven Jesuit Scholastics Who Spent a Month in the Diocese

GENERAL OBSERVATIONS

Our review of our work-and-life experience with various communities of the diocese was based on the relationship between the gospel and life as the criterion for an evaluation of the communities with which we became acquainted.

It seems to us that this relationship between the gospel and life, though quite real to the pastoral ministers (community directors), has not yet sunk deeply into every community and the whole community (for example, in Pitombeira). This is concretely reflected in the type of celebration and religious education one finds in these communities, as well as in their failure to join in the struggle for the organization of the people and for the repossession of their land (for example, in the union movement).

There is great effort on the part of the directors to incarnate and demonstrate the relationship between the gospel and life. But the participation of the people in general is still relatively weak in certain locales. We note that the ones involved in many community activities are mostly women, senior citizens, and children, with young persons, especialiy, absent.

In some localities the presence of the directors does launch the process of integration between gospel and life. Still, we wonder whether the danger may exist of falling into a dependence on a "pastoral elite"—of having the whole development of the communities depend on certain individuals.

We likewise note that the process of integration between gospel and life is always easier (or less difficult) in the lower social strata— among wage-earners and workers—and harder for small land-owners.

As for the various levels of integration between the gospel and life, we seem to see a relationship between the tools that are used in the ministry (Bible groups, celebrations, workers' meetings, and so on) and the personal options and work methods of the persons directing the communities (especially priests and religious). For example, Bishop Fragoso prefers the movement for nonviolence, Frédy uses the Suffering Servant meetings, and so on. Here the question would be: What impact do these personal options have on the awareness of the people? To what extent are these just personal options and to what extent can they bring the people to take the same path? Could they cause a certain amount of confusion, by making a personal option look like that of the whole diocese? What are the repercussions of these options for the political question properly so called—political parties, and so on?

Dom Fragoso's arrival in Crateús, and the new approach to the pastoral ministry, coincided with the coup of 1964 and the emergence of the most varied forms of repression of the popular movements. Accordingly, it seems to us, in many localities the acceptance of the diocesan pastoral approach is impeded by the alienation forced on the people, and by the ideological bombardment to which the masses are subjected (fear of communism is still very strong in some places). Despite these difficulties (and so many others), Dom Fragoso's efforts to adapt to the rhythm of the communities, and to try to be the point of unity of the diocese, is eminently laudable.

We also note that the diocese has, if not an "option," then a certain preference, at any rate, for using "legal ways" to try to help solve the most serious of the social problems: the question of the land. Its recommendation of the unions, with all the limitations imposed on these by current law, its implementation (rediscovery!) of the Land Statute, actually somewhat passé, are expressions of this preference or concern. Our question: Is this a positive strategy, or is it merely the "only way to go" because other routes are blocked? Are the independent popular organizations an end to be attained or are they out of the question? Will there be a movement in this direction? Should one be started?

As for the CPT, the Land Pastoral Commission, we note that its activity has been excellent and decisive in those localities where the population is already organized in one way or another to confront its problems. We recognize that there is a great deal of work to be done right here, but we wonder whether the CPT should perhaps concern itself more with other localities, where popular organization is further behind.

As for bringing in experts or pastoral workers from outside the diocese—like ourselves, for instance, who have spent only one month in the communities and who are not very familiar with the situation, or others who go there for a shorter or longer time—our question is: If the presence of outsiders is acknowledged as useful, what role are they expected to play in the communities? What is the role of the Diocesan Pastoral Council, and even of the communities, in preparing and assisting these outsiders, lest they have a negative influence on the process developed in the communities? We consider it very important for the communities to share in the decision of whether to accept outsiders or not, and to help formulate the conditions for their acceptance.

Finally, the general impression we have had of the diocese of Crateús has been extremely positive. Its recognition and encouragement of the base-level communities, participation by the people in pastoral decisions (through the Diocesan Pastoral Council), the people's participation in the popular movements, the new image of the priest and bishop, their adoption of the people's living conditions, getting beyond assistentialism and the paucity of resources— all this and so much more have projected a new image of the church, giving great hope to anyone with eyes open to read the signs of the times and ears to hear what the Spirit is saying to the churches.

OBSERVATIONS ON THE SANTO ANTÔNIO COMMUNITY

This Christian community is not yet a real expression of Christian life. The director, *animador,* has little preparation and no interest in leading the others along a path of involvement in the situation in which they live. He becomes an instrument of domination, by reason both of the place he occupies in the community and his status as a large landholder, and takes advantage of his opportunity to further his political and economic interests.

The communities round about have been completely forgotten, and only now, with the formation of a group of religion teachers, have children begun to be prepared for their first communion. The presence of the diocese in the locality is practically nil, and this has contributed to a great religious ignorance. Any real expression of religion is all but absent.

This region is remarkable for the proliferation of groups of Evangelicals who increasingly impose their religious view on the people, thus causing difficulties for the work of conscientization.

The practical absence of the diocese here, and the lack of communication with those in charge of the community, rendered our work difficult during the time we were there, and our presence was not really looked on as having anything to do with the diocese. To our way of thinking, the only vital representation of the Christian community there is its group of catechists, and we think that in the present situation this group could be the starting point for real progress.

OBSERVATIONS ON THE MONTE NEBO COMMUNITY

This area has been relatively unaffected by the drought. It also has more advanced farm equipment. The large and middle-size landholders have modern machinery, and this should be taken into account in any analysis of the internal tensions of the community. Most of the land is farmed, and even the landless tenants lease tractors and pay in kind.

There are two predominant families in the community, one of them owning very extensive tracts, the other owning middle-size ones. Then there are the small landowners and landless tenants.

The large and medium-size landowners are in control not only of the economics of the area, but of the politics and religion as well.

The *animadores* are middle-size landowners, and the Christian community is made up of their peers. The *animadores* are well trained, but owing to family ties are often the tools of the large landowners. As a result, although their activity is directed to the very poorest, it is limited to preparation for the reception of the sacraments, or celebrations without much political content in the way of motivation for a struggle for better living conditions. The participation of small landowners or tenant farmers is greatly reduced in the community, so that there is a certain separation between the religious expressions of either group. In the little time we spent in the community, we were able to observe that the language of the *animadores,* though expressing liberative content, is unrelated to the concrete problems of the community.

The participation of youth is minimal. We think more work should be done with them, with the future development of the community in mind.

We also think that the parish pastoral team could be doing more here, not only with the *animadores,* but with the whole community. This could lead to a clearer detection of community tensions, and especially to a greater participation in the community by the very poorest.

OBSERVATIONS ON THE SANTO ANDRÉ COMMUNITY

Some 120 families live in the community of Santo André, scattered along the road. The core of the community is made up of some thirty families living near the director, *animadora*. For the most part, the community is made up of middle-size and small landowners working their own lands, some using hired hands.

The community is engaged in farming a community plantation, and has been doing so for five years. The grandfather of the *animadora* gave the community two hectares of land to plant maize and beans. By January, under the direction of the *animadora,* twenty-five persons had already prepared the fields and were only waiting for the rains so that they could do the planting. The money the crop will bring in is earmarked for a first-aid station in the locality.

The workers' union meets every two weeks or once a month in the director's house. Most of the members are proprietors, and some have farm hands working for them. One of the biggest problems facing the union is absenteeism at union meetings and failure to pay dues.

Celebrations of the word are prepared by the director with the help of a group of girls. The celebration is in a different house every Sunday, because there is no permanent place available. Some fifty persons participate.

Santo André seems to us to be a very dynamic community, with the participation of a great number of young persons, which makes it possible to do very fruitful pastoral work. The director, *animadora,* is full of enthusiasm, and her leadership is unquestioningly accepted by all. The future of the community is certainly promising, as long as the director takes the right direction and has adequate help. She will need a great deal of support where the community plantation is concerned, as well as in the struggle being waged by the community with the prefecture for the improvement of education in the locality.

OBSERVATIONS ON THE PITOMBEIRA EXPERIMENT

As to the impact of this experiment on our personal training, we must say that it was powerful, and for several reasons.

First, we became acquainted with the reality of farm life. We shared the daily life of the *camponeses* in their concrete day-to-day difficulties, in their lack of resources with which to better their living conditions, and in their condition of exploitation by political and economic structures of domination. It was most impressive for us to come to know the situation of the *camponeses* at close range, and the insecurity they have to live in. They have usucapient title to their fields (they say *uso campeão* "championship use," instead of *usucapião,* "right of ownership based on uninterrupted use for many years"). But they know that they are under constant danger of losing their property because of the ruthless tactics of land speculators.

Secondly, we have seen vast possibilities for apostolic work there, real possibilities for labor in the service of faith and justice. Our experiences living with farm people have shown us very concrete uses for our charism here, a new way of being a Jesuit, working in the fields, as our confrere Paco is doing right now [see part 3, chapter 1, above].

Thirdly, for Mota, one of us seven, whose roots are here in this rural area, this was an especially rich period in motivation, and in new elements for a more critical apostolic discernment. The experience of coming back here and living again with his people, in service to the people, has led him to question the manner of preparation for this kind of service, and to come to grips with the apostolic priorities of the Society of Jesus here in Nordeste today.

OBSERVATIONS ON PACO'S ROLE IN PITOMBEIRA

As far as the province is concerned, there is the impression that Paco's experiment is temporary. It is not very well accepted by some Jesuits of the province.

Paco's full involvement in the people's real situation is supremely positive, not because it validates (shows the real value already existing in) the life of the people, which it does, but because it shows a new image of the priest and the church, one involving an option for the poor. One of the most rewarding aspects of our practicum was the opportunity to become aware of the people's "rhythm," and the efforts of a new pedagogy of the faith, which is leading the people little by little to perceive the true dimensions and implications of the priesthood of the faithful.

Secondly, the testimony of an austere life is most positive. It shows a pastoral minister's consistency with an option made for the poor, as it manifests this option in a radical simplicity of life. This way of living facilitates the sharing of life experiences, facilitates a mutual understanding with the faithful, who feel closer to the priest, and feel that it is a good and worthy thing to be a *camponês*. They see it in the person of the priest toiling in the fields on their communal plantation.

Thirdly, it would seem to be important to be on the lookout for incentives to the people's creativity in the development of new forms of community work.

Finally, the question of providing for oneself raises a question about Paco, even for the people. Isn't he doing without essentials, placing his health, and thereby his continued work, at risk? Some of the people have asked Mota to call his attention to this point.

OBSERVATIONS ON COMMUNITY PRIORITIES IN PITOMBEIRA

The process of community maturation is still very slow, as indeed it must be.

We feel a need to provide an incentive for the training of new leaders. Creuza, the present leader, is more and more overburdened.

There are still certain paternalistic expectations on the part of the people with regard to the priest, and it will be important to be careful here. The case is similar with community leaders whose dynamism and creativity are such that they may take up room that ought to be opened to others.

Political conscientization and union organizing present a great problem. It will be important to encourage leaders to come forward from among the workers. It will likewise be important to provide an incentive for more participation by all in dealing with questions that concern all. The problems involved in the land questions are becoming more serious with the passage of time, and there will have to be more organization if these problems are to be faced.

It would be ideal to seek more contact with communities with experience in this area, and to share with them the difficulties felt when it comes to organizing.

Another problem is the situation of young persons in the community. Boys do not participate very much in community activities. Nor, perhaps because they expect to move on, are they much involved in the struggles of the people of the locality.

We think that the question of the reorganization of political parties ought to be discussed with the people. This is the right moment to broach the political question, and help the people raise its consciousness above an attitude of paternalism toward political figures and take a more active and demanding part in this sphere.

OBSERVATIONS ON THE COMMUNITY IN MONSENHOR TABOSA

The union. The government favors two types of union. One is composed of employers, from the small landowners with a few employees to the largest ranchers. The other is made up of small farmers, sharecroppers, and hired hands. The union of this latter type numbers some three thousand members in Monsenhor Tabosa. About 120 workers come to the monthly meetings. All members are assessed 10 cruzeiros a month in dues, and this gives them the right to free medical consultation. In town, there are other union delegations, and these advocate meetings by zones.

The Monsenhor Tabosa union has the reputation of being a fighter. At the moment its president has only very limited opportunities to achieve anything worthwhile. There is confusion about medical insurance and union membership, owing to the way the government started the unions and structured them in the first place. A further difficulty lies in the variety of concerns among the membership. Joint action is very difficult in these circumstances. At the moment the union leadership is in the hands of the small farmers. The main object of their battle at the moment is a just rent for the land they work. Legally they are supposed to pay 10 percent of their proceeds, but in fact 20 percent is collected. Secondarily, they are waging a struggle for the land itself, and for an independent union with its own rules and regulations. These three demands were the subject of the meeting of thirty-five hundred farm workers in Brasília this past year.

All this is a picture of the union as seen through the eyes of its president.

There is discontent with the union among certain elements of the membership. The main reasons are as follows. A great deal of importance is attached to interest rates and the question of credit administration. The official leadership of the union almost never varies. It has been held by practically the same persons for eight years now. The attitude of this leadership is passive and legalistic. Those in charge wait to be approached by the membership with problems; they take no initiative themselves. When any action is taken it is always within the strict bounds set by the government. Although the union has its own attorney, no confidence is placed in him or his ability to actually defend the interests of the workers.

The parish team. During the years when the people were without a pastor, a group of lay persons took the initiative in keeping up pastoral activities. For a while they had the help of two North American religious, women who lived with the people and carried out the first steps in the preparation of groups for the reception of the sacraments. They also met with youth groups. It has been from these latter that the present CEBs have arisen. Some of these lay persons belong today to the parish team that was formed when Hidenori arrived in the parish.

Members of this team have had some experience. But as a team they are only just starting out, and have not gotten a great deal going yet, but the team has fine potential. We were able to participate in some meetings to prepare for Christmas, the patronal feast, meetings of community leaders, meetings of representatives of youth groups, regional reviews of work accomplished, and so on. We were struck by the amount of participation in the planning, execution, and evaluation of the various activities, and by the depth of reflection on work undertaken and the questions about it. In all this the attitude taken by Hidenori has been a great help.

The rectory is really a community building. Everyone who goes there feels at home—mainly the members of the parish team, the *animadores* of the communities, and their members. The people can remember when the rectory was the pastor's home, visited only by the rich, and where the poor had no desire to go, because they were afraid.

The union president and secretary are on the parish team. From the standpoint of *church support for the union movement* this is important, because it promotes cooperation and understanding. It also presents some ambiguities. You don't hear the criticisms that are made of the union when it comes to the written evaluation that the community leaders are supposed to submit in preparation for the evaluation and planning meeting. There may be a certain identification between church and union by reason of the presence of two union leaders on the parish team, so that community leaders feel reticent when it comes to expressing criticism. Passivity at the leadership level has engendered passivity in the union membership, and the confusion to which we have referred is scarcely of any help in the matter.

Our reflections in our first meeting on the option of the church with regard to political and union affairs touched on this point very directly. Among the ambiguities to be corrected in the process, we consider the appearance, or continuation, of a legalistic mentality to be an important one. The masses trust the law, and ascribe any unfairness to the corruption of local authorities, thinking that all they have to do is appeal to federal statutes. "The law of the state defends the *camponês*," they say.

Finances. The church of the poor does not find economic matters easy, especially because this is an element open to manipulation by large landholders and business leaders. They are very much in sight when it comes to underwriting the cost of public religious celebrations, although neither hide nor hair of them is in evidence in other parish activities and celebrations. This reinforces an image of generosity and legitimacy in an exploiter, and presents an obstacle to a critical analysis by the *camponeses* of their situation.

Image of the bishop. There is a real awareness that Dom Fragoso is on the side of the poor and supports them. This is reinforced by the stories that circulate to the effect that there is friction between him and the wealthy, and that he has been accused of communism. This gives the poor a great deal of security. They no longer feel alone. Having the church on their side lends an aura of legitimacy to their struggle. Similarly, the kind of presence that Hidenori has brought to the community has also begun to produce its first results. The *camponeses* can see that he is very good and generous, and that he is studying to be a priest. They see that he lives with them and lives as they do. And so they get to know him better and he gets to know the real parish situation better.

Community Dynamics. The objective of the communities is a life lived in common through a shared faith and through a response to the problems that present themselves in daily life. The communities constitute authentic forms of popular organization. Organized in this way, the communities reflect on their own ongoing process, their challenges, and their failures. In this way, the communities are a means of reflection and joint action from a starting point in faith.

Each community has its own story. Each has its own way of constructing a synthesis of faith and life. This is what the great effort of all the communities consists in. They try to discover a living faith through the quest for justice in their mutual relationships and their conditions of economic productivity. Not all communities achieve the same level of faith expression. There is an enormous variety in the communities. Some have just begun; others have been in existence for several years. Generally speaking, the degree of politico-social awareness manifested by a community from a starting point in the union between faith and life is greater in communities that have existed for some time, and where more vital, vigorous activity has developed. There are communities in which faith becomes explicit in the building of a chapel, whereas in others living the faith means supporting and defending the members of the community who are exploited by large landholders.

Communities are the place where, through a fairly democratic structure, the *camponeses* take on community responsibilities, discussing their problems, and all of them having an opportunity to share and be heard—the place where they launch their initiatives for community progress, and interpret scripture from a point of departure in their own lives. This makes the communities a means of popular education for the *camponeses,* so that they gradually achieve a higher level of commitment on the part of their members, and consequently a more critical and democratic awareness of the possibilities and importance of social interaction. This enables them to identify injustice more easily and act against it.

The multiformity among communities is also evidenced in the form, the frequency, and the variety of occasions on which they meet. There are newly-formed communities that express their dynamics in a weekly meeting. Others, engaged in more highly developed processes, come together in several weekly meetings of the various groups of which they are composed—women, youth, groups preparing for the celebration of the sacraments, and so on—and meet as a community only once a month, while carrying on a multiplicity of community activities for the purpose of improving their economic conditions, such as common vegetable gardens, a community plantation, a co-op, or small shops.

Within the communities, some members develop a profound awareness of their "evangelizing" responsibility. Many of these individuals have created and trained new communities in neighboring, or even distant, regions. It is very common to find present at meetings visitors desirous of lending additional thrust to the process of the community they are visiting as well as their own, through an exchange of experiences. These individuals are keenly aware of the wealth of a living faith, which has taken root in them through the communities, and they make several trips a week to proclaim their discoveries. A good example of this kind of person is to be found in many *animadores.*

All this imposes on the parish an obligation to intensify its help in the developmental process of each community. Of course, the parish team tries to be present in the life of its communities by coordinating the work of the community *animadores* and youth groups. But this is not enough. Closer cooperation is needed, and it should be based on plans worked out from the concrete situation of each community. Until now, this support has consisted in the participation by some members of the communities in activities or meetings set up by the parish in the municipality of Monsenhor Tabosa. What is needed now is the presence of the parish team within the communities themselves, to provide a thrust for their dynamism from a point of departure in each one's own situation.

Sacramental ministry. There should be a more thorough preparation for first communion, marriage, baptisms, and reconciliation. Certainly something has been achieved in the new approaches that help so much to make persons more aware of the value of the sacraments and their meaning for life. Still, preparation for the celebration of these sacraments is set up outside the life of the communities, with the result that it must be more a mass ministry than a personal and personalizing one. The opposite occurs with confirmation and first communion when these are prepared for in the communities themselves. These sacraments then become dynamizing elements fostering personal growth in faith, and hence in commitment to the community.

Germano	*Marcelo*	*José*
Joaquim	*Mota*	*Gabriel*
Alfredo		

3

SOME FRIENDLY QUESTIONS
FOR THE DIOCESE OF CRATEÚS

Sister Jane, Pastoral Animadora *in Monsenhor Tabosa,
Poranga, and Pé de Serra, and Member of the CPT*

I believe that the diocesan church of Crateús—the people as well
as the pastoral ministers, the bishop, and the priests—has a dream:
"This church of ours should be the church of the oppressed people,
the church of Jesus Christ alive in today's world, a world so full of
injustice, oppression, and inequality." Still, in my experience, we
don't really take hold of this dream. We never "articulate" for one
another this dream of ours. We never put right out there on the
table what we've dreamt together.

Wouldn't it be fun to articulate this dream, to put it right out
there on the table?

Not having articulated this dream, we haven't managed to trans-
late it into clear, concrete objectives taken up and understood by
all.

Not having clear, concrete objectives taken up and understood
by all, we've found it hard to define concrete steps and then take
these steps as a group, in order to make our dream reality. Nor do
we talk about establishing priorities.

Even our language betrays us. Often our words are the same, but what is meant by these words is very different.

For lack of an objective and priorities, established jointly, I wonder if we don't have a tendency to just take up *everything,* every kind of charism and work. In one way this openness is something very positive. But at the same time it often appears to me that this "taking on tasks" is more on a personal level than a group level. And so we run the risk of generating a series of problems that can slow down the journey we're making with the people and cause difficulties along the way. I'm not talking about the variety of charisms and tasks; I'm talking about the way we take them up that can cause difficulties.

Not having clear objectives and priorities, established jointly, what can our diocesan structures express?

DIOCESAN PASTORAL COUNCIL

We're constantly reminding ourselves and one another that the people, the grass roots, the "base," must share in the workings of the Diocesan Pastoral Council. I think that popular participation in the diocesan church is a value accepted by all. Still, I wonder if popular participation in the council the way it is today actually realizes this value. In my concrete experience, (1) the council structure comes from above, without any room for lay persons to express themselves as far as their needs, their problems, their struggle, is concerned; and (2) this is because the matters taken up by the council aren't those of the people, don't treat of the life of the people but of the problems of our structures—the parishes, and so on.

Concretely, what does the council, the way it is today, have to do with the people's journey?

What happens to an individual from the grass roots who participates in the workings of the council the way it is today? Doesn't he or she run the risk of being frustrated by old, worn-out structures?

We make an effort, but we don't actually succeed, generally, in sharing and evaluating our base-level experiences. We don't really evaluate together our pedagogical methodology in the light of clear criteria and objectives accepted by all. To a certain extent, this difficulty prevents us from profiting and learning from the experiences of others. It also presents an obstacle to a kind of joint apprenticeship.

DIOCESAN ADMINISTRATIVE COUNCIL

Again, for lack of objectives and priorities in common, in pastoral terms what are the pastoral and pedagogical criteria for our financial and administrative decisions?

PARISH STRUCTURES

The journey of the church, of the people in its quest for liberation and a new world, extends beyond the boundaries of a parish, a municipality, or a diocese. But we have the tendency to isolate ourselves in parish structures, in the liturgical and sacramental areas as well as in the area of struggle.

What is the effect of this "parochial" tendency of ours on the people's struggle and journey?

Why do grassroots teams that don't follow this traditional, parochial style not last long in the diocese?

I offer these reflections not by way of judging anyone, but just to stimulate questions and offer any help I can along the road. I hope it helps. This is how I mean it.

4

THE STRUCTURE
OF OUR DIOCESE

Sister Lemos, Animadora *in Parambu, Poranga, Pé de Serra, and* Nova *Russas, and Member of the Pastoral Campaign Coordinating Committee*

Saying anything about the structure of the diocese costs me sweat and blood. But I'll try to make a contribution by saying what I think.

In the *first place,* I'd like to mention what's *good.*

It's not a heavy, rigid structure, with minute, rigid criteria for the teams and community leaders, expecting them to accept whatever directives are handed down from above. The parishes are autonomous when it comes to meeting the needs they find and serving the people. For example: preparation for the sacraments, area meetings, teams, communities.

The diocesan structure requires parish teams to make a joint presentation of what they're doing for the grass roots. This is good. It helps them keep their minds on finding the path the journey should take. Each parish has already defined, or at least feels the need of defining, its objectives.

On the other hand, there are some negative points:

1. Too much flexibility can shatter the unity of the whole in

certain respects. It often seems as if the strands come undone. What I mean is that we don't have a well-defined objective in the diocese that would consolidate the journey of all the parishes, starting at the grass roots.

A question: Isn't it time to concretize this objective, starting out with what already exists in the parishes and with the grass roots, and putting it all together?

Everyone here understands the *option* of the diocese for the oppressed. This option is clearly defined. We seek a free, just society of sisters and brothers, in which every one will have *voz e vez,* voice and vote. But as an *objective* this isn't definite and clear in everyone's mind. There should be more "joint defining," by leaders and grass roots together. At least this is how I see it.

Wouldn't this be the reason why there are individuals who don't know where they're going and don't have a place? This presents a difficulty for the grassroots journey, which we want to help make its way forward.

2. We have no mechanism for facilitating an amalgamation of the base-level communities with one another, some way of offering them room to express themselves and be heard. And some way of getting community representatives to bring up the needs and thinking of their fellows instead of their own.

3. As for the Diocesan Pastoral Council, we have to have an organ in the diocese for representation and decision. As it currently operates, there isn't room for base-level members. The problems treated are important and necessary, all right, but not for them. I don't mean that they don't see the importance of what's discussed or reflected on. But they have to be able to speak for their fellow community members, and they need room to be able to do this. What can be done? Light is beginning to dawn. In the last council meeting, this was discussed. Vistas are opening up, ideas are coming. It's up to all of us to move ahead with what was discussed and decided there.

The seed has been sown. Many signs are springing up from this seed—communities are starting up and beginning to move ahead on their journey. There are signs of autonomy, organization, solidarity with others, awareness of one's dignity, and a struggle for justice and rights.

The journey is slow, but it's moving.

5

NOTES FOR A PORTRAIT
OF THE CHURCH OF CRATEÚS

*Father Eliésio dos Santos, Pastor in Parambu
and Crateús, and Member of the Diocesan Pastoral
Coordinating Committee*

INTRODUCTION

Others have spoken of the structural and programatic organization of the local church of Crateús. Without clear, careful attention to this, we shall make no progress. Without visible, discernible forms in which to express ourselves, we shall not be able to express an evangelical, ecclesial testimony. When all is said and done, it is precisely our way of living with one another, and celebrating and proclaiming the kingdom, that will reveal our boundless hope, our passionate love that unites, reconciles, and builds a new earth and a new heaven, based on *freedom* exercised in democracy, and projected toward its ultimate form—the kingdom where there will be no more weeping, struggle, or death.

I shall speak of other points, however, which are not to be forgotten in this broad discussion now being undertaken by the church of Crateús. Let me begin by saying that I am most happy to have had the good fortune to share in this journey of a church, so full of challenges and adventures, for nearly ten years now. I have been a witness of this church, which inspired me to be a priest in its service, and for that I have never been sorry.

THE PATH TO SELF-UNDERSTANDING

Church of the rich. We live a church life whose faith reference has been bound up with a consistent commitment to human beings impoverished by an unjust system of distribution of goods and access to opportunities. Faith in Jesus Christ had led the faithful to fervor, piety, and even to relevant deeds of charity. But their understanding had not yet been able to embrace the structural, radical dimension of social injustice, the fruit of sin. A devotional spirit led them to build and be zealous for the church as temple. The first places in the pews, their names on the columns, elaborate mausoleums, and so on, belonged to those who had contributed the most to the sumptuousness of the edifice.

The poor regarded all of this with a certain admiration, but had neither voice nor vote in it. It is no exaggeration to say that this church, for obvious reasons, was the cultural expression of those who had built it, directed it, and then controlled it. Attempts by the poor to formulate their faith out of their own, peripheral, culture were considered out of place and superstitious. Their ministers were nearly always recruited from the families who controlled the church. This type of church is still the soporific model dear to many hearts.

Church on the side of the poor. In 1971, after a door-to-door visit of the extensive parish of Tauá (suffering from the expulsion of its pastor, Father José Pedândola), Father Frédy told us, in a meeting of the Pastoral Council, "The parishioners say that their priest was expelled from Tauá because he took the side of the poor." Perhaps those who made this statement did not realize how historic a pronouncement they were making. This was an exact formulation of the new understanding of church emerging at that time: a church on the side of the poor.

Those of us who have felt what it is to take this step have seen and felt the solidity and strength it has. Priests and pastoral ministers are suddenly recognized as a church on the side of the poor.

This notion has been expressed in forms of sacrifice, self-denial, and heroism the value of whose testimony we shall never be able fully to measure. How many weary journeys over country roads, how many sleepless nights of conflict, how much effort to live with one's sisters and brothers in simplicity, never to be recorded in the archives, in the chronicles of this church! This had all been indispensable for preparing the rich soil from which a third self-understanding of church would spring.

Church of the poor. A new self-understanding of church seems to be taking shape, in vigorous lines indeed, on our horizon. Everywhere is heard, in the mouth of the communities that arise in the midst of the poor, "The Church? That's us!" This stage of awareness seems to me to be one of great importance. The church no longer appears as a foreign organism that might, at most, take up the cause of the poor and take a stand for them. The church has actually allowed itself to be absorbed by the poor. The poor discover themselves to be church. This is the great novelty of this stage of ecclesial self-comprehension. And so the poor have begun to express their opinions on the organization of the church, the ministry of priests and bishops, and all services rendered or to be rendered by the church.

AN OLD MAN, A YOUNG WOMAN, AND A CHILD

There lived in Jerusalem at the time a certain man named Simeon. He was just and pious, and awaited the consolation of Israel, and the Holy Spirit was upon him. It was revealed to him by the Holy Spirit that he would not experience death until he had seen the Anointed of the Lord. He came to the temple now, inspired by the Spirit, and when the parents brought in the child Jesus to perform for him the customary ritual of the law, he took him in his arms and blessed God in these words:

"Now, Master, you can dismiss your servant in peace;
    you have fulfilled your word.
For my eyes have witnessed your saving deed
    displayed for all the peoples to see:
A revealing light to the Gentiles,
    the glory of your people Israel."

The child's father and mother were marveling at what was being said about him. Simeon blessed them and said to Mary his mother: "This child is destined to be the downfall and the rise of many in Israel, a sign that will be opposed—and you yourself shall be pierced with a sword—so that the thoughts of many hearts may be laid bare" [Luke 2:25-35].

This reading from Luke, an expression of faith of the poor of Yahweh at that time, and our own reading of the experience of a church born of the people by the action of the Holy Spirit today have certain points of convergence:

Salvation is defined in the text of Luke as the historical consolation of Israel. The name of the salvation being accomplished in the history of our continent and celebrated by the poor is liberation, in contradistinction to the historical oppression by which they are crushed.

Three times, in three consecutive verses in this text, we read of the Holy Spirit. God is the author of the might of Pentecost, the basis of liberation, a God who acts in breadth and depth, and excludes from regeneration no person, no structure, no organization.

When all is said and done, the power of God prevails.

The conflictuality of the liberation process is characterized as a combat of the forces of evil with God.

The hope of Simeon, old and poor, now in the twilight of his life, the weakness of a woman, already so crushed by a male-dominated society, the vulnerability of a defenseless child—these are the apparatus mounted by God against the forces of evil. A self-consistent understanding of a church of the poor cannot neglect these indications. What we call "poor means of evangelization" are perhaps deserving of much more meditation.

PROBLEMS TO SOLVE

In a Bible course in Nova Russas, a *camponês* expressed his understanding of God's dream for a new world in the following words: "God's dream is that we all get to eating off the same plate." His reflection grew out of his observation that the rich eat their own portion, and then they eat the portion of the poor as well, leaving the latter in misery. The poor have intuited the universality of God's plan for liberation in Jesus Christ. The problem is how to bring this universal dimension of liberation—the full expression of the love of the Lord for the people—to an in-depth realization in liberation practice itself.

The transition from a church on the side of the poor to a church of the poor entails an identity crisis for pastoral ministers. For the people to come to expression and self-determination, the pastoral minister must withdraw. There is no other way. The hierarchy has so long been an instrument of domination in the people's eyes! The problem here is one of courageous realism. How should our activity as pastoral ministers be shaped in this historical moment of such importance for the emergence of a new face of the church?

Obviously a church born of the people, of the poor, by the action of the Holy Spirit, will not be able to continue to recruit its ministers, its servants, as it did before. This leads me to believe that it is urgent to rethink, together with the communities, our criteria for the recruitment and training of new ministers. This discussion will not be an easy one, and that alone makes it urgent for the church to begin it, and not only locally, but regionally and across the continent as well.

A product of this ecclesial self-understanding should be the re-creation of a spirituality in depth to provide support along the journey. A theology of liberation—an attempt to bring the data of faith into confrontation with historical mediations, with a view to a liberation practice—is not enough. The spirituality of liberation will steer our passion, too, our affectivity, our deepest attitudes, our experience, toward the God who, out of love, has decided to strike an alliance with the people and together with the people win total, definitive, irrevocable freedom.

A PRAYER

Lord, the church of the poor is a mystery of faith. It is not by human means that we shall come to believe that the promised liberation will come from a poor, defenseless infant lying on straw.

Lord, the might of the poor is a mystery of faith. It is not by human means that we shall come to believe that defeated, torn, crucified human being will clear a path to a new, free, reconciled world.

Lord, the liberation of the poor is a mystery of faith. It is not by human means that we shall come to believe that a corpse three days dead would come to be raised again, as guarantee, anticipation, and certitude that it is not useless to believe in the impossible, for God makes it possible.

Help this local church of Crateús, this pilgrim church, believe in the mystery of your poverty, believe in the strength that comes from a passion undergone for love, and confidently expect liberation of all men and women, but especially of the ill-treated, downtrodden, and humiliated of this earth.

Fill the heart of this church with tender mercy, to receive all men and women into a dialogue of brothers and sisters redeemed and washed by the blood of your Son, who still sheds the layer of the offering of the poor on a world he intends to lead to freedom.

Amen.

6

SISTER ABIGAIL AND THE LIBERATOR GOD

Father Alfredo (Frédy) Kunz, of the Sons of Charity,
Member of the Crateús Parish Team

To all of the members of the church of Crateús, committed to the poor, I wish peace and joy in the Lord.

In this report I simply want to talk about what seems to me to have been the greatest event in the life of the diocese of Crateús since 1964.

In 1975 the members of the Diocesan Pastoral Commission, together with their bishop, Dom Fragoso, sent Sister Abigail, newly arrived from the state of Minas Gerais, to live with the *camponeses* of the church of São Gonçalo, in the district of Ipueiras.

A daring experiment had been under way in this region—a cooperative, in which the diocese had invested its best personnel. But then the project had to be abandoned. The community, like its tractor, was idled by a flat tire.

Gloom prevailed.

Then Sister Abigail arrived, without a cent, saying, "I'm not on the 'project,' I only came to live here—to pray and work with you."

Then she fixed up a house, and arranged a room for the Blessed Sacrament. She fixed up a wooden bucket and went to fetch water. She fixed up a mattock and went to work on the plantation. She changed clothes and went to visit the neighbors.

And that's what she does today. Her life hasn't changed. She works, she prays, she lives with the very poorest.

But the community of São Gonçalo has changed.

Gradually, in contact with this sister who spoke their language, and moved by her simple manner of life, the poor discovered their own value, and began to organize, without any money or equipment.

In that year the diocese unwittingly anticipated the vision of Puebla. In that prophetic hour, in the person of Abigail, the diocese began its conversion.

In the Final Document of the Puebla meeting of the bishops of Latin America, we read:

CONVERSION OF THE CHURCH

In order to live and proclaim the demand of Christian poverty, the church today will need to *review its structures* and the *life of all its members,* especially its pastoral ministers, with a view to a genuine conversion. Once converted, it will be able effectively to evangelize the poor [italics added].

In view of the extreme poverty of Latin America, the Final Document has this to say:

This conversion will entail an austere lifestyle, and total confidence in the Lord. The church, in its evangelizing activity, will rely more on *God's being, power, and grace,* than on having more resources, or on secular power. Thus the church will present an image that is authentically poor, open to God, and ever available to its brothers and sisters. In this church, the poor will have the real opportunity to *participate,* and to be recognized for their real worth [italics added].

When I arrived in Crateús in 1968, many ways of living the gospel in the historical context of Latin America were revealed to me. For example, there was human promotion, grassroots education, the liberation struggle, the struggle for justice, political education, the union movement and class organization, the struggle for land reform, Christian involvement in conflicts over land ownership, and so on.

Today I can see the face of the committed and courageous brothers or sisters at the head of every one of those movements. Crateús tries to live an incarnate gospel. This is a sign of the good health of the diocese. Can anyone doubt the value of the type of example given by a life like Abigail's.

Gandhi used to say: "Personal reform or self-purification is a hundred times more dear to my heart than so-called political activity."

Is our vision of the liberation of the human being really total? When do we ever speak, seriously, of *our own interior liberation from the passions?* What change can possibly bring economic liberation to our country if Brazilians, before and after, make no attempt to liberate themselves from consumerism?

In various dioceses of Brazil there are meetings and retreats conducted by regular directors, generally priests or religious, who live in the little base-level communities, for example in Recife, João Pessoa, and so on.

Some nine individuals in the diocese live Abigail's lifestyle. What place is accorded them in the whole picture? Are they not somewhat marginalized? Why?

How can we help them improve their prayer life, be more present to the community they have chosen, live more intimately with the poor?

Why have they not been more skillful at sensitizing us?

Before sending Moses to liberate the Jews from the power of pharaoh of Egypt, the Lord spoke from the midst of the bush:

"Come no nearer! Remove the sandals from your feet, for the place where you stand is holy ground. I am the God of your father, the God of Abraham, the God of Isaac, the God of Jacob." Moses hid his face, for he was afraid to look at God [Exodus 3:5-6].

Our battle for the liberation of the integral human being must begin with an encounter with the living God, Jesus, the only savior.

As I see it, this is what the diocese meant when, in 1975, it sent Abigail, with only the clothes on her back, to the mountaintop.

Once upon a time a daughter of Israel sang, good and loud, in a land occupied by troops of the Emperor Caesar Augustus: "He has deposed the mighty from their thrones and raised the lowly to high places" (Luke 1:52). She was carrying the Liberator God with her.